Campaigning Online

Bruce Bimber and Richard Davis

Campaigning

Online

The Internet in U.S. Elections

OXFORD
UNIVERSITY PRESS

2003

OXFORD
UNIVERSITY PRESS

Oxford   New York
Auckland   Bangkok   Buenos Aires   Cape Town   Chennai
Dar es Salaam   Delhi   Hong Kong   Istanbul   Karachi   Kolkata
Kuala Lumpur   Madrid   Melbourne   Mexico City   Mumbai   Nairobi
São Paulo   Shanghai   Taipei   Tokyo   Toronto

Copyright © 2003 by Oxford University Press, Inc.

Published by Oxford University Press, Inc.
198 Madison Avenue, New York, New York 10016

www.oup.com

Oxford is a registered trademark of Oxford University Press

Library of Congress Cataloging-in-Publication Data
Bimber, Bruce A. (Bruce Allen), 1961–
Campaigning online : the Internet in U.S. elections / by Bruce Bimber
and Richard Davis.
    p. cm.
Includes index.
ISBN 0-19-515155-0; 0-19-515156-9 (pbk.)
1. Internet in political campaigns—United States.
2. Elections—United States—Computer network resources.
I. Davis, Richard, 1955–   II. Title.
JK2281 .B56 2003
324.7'3—dc21   2002151777

9 8 7 6 5 4 3 2

Printed in the United States of America
on acid-free paper

To my wife, Laura (B.B.)

To my wife, Molina (R.D.)

.

Contents

Figures and Tables

Figures

Tables

Figures and Tables

Campaigning Online

[The Internet] was our ultimate means of communication with people.
Jonah Baker, Webmaster, Nader Campaign for President, 2000

Not only is [the Internet] a message tool but . . . it is a coordination tool. It allows
you to coordinate a nationwide campaign from headquarters.
Cliff Angelo, E-Campaign Coordinator, Bush Campaign for President, 2000

The rules of campaigning since the beginning of the TV era are still in play.
Lynn Reed, Internet Director, Bradley Campaign for President, 2000

The Question: Reinforcement or Renewal?

In the realm of American democracy, the year 2000 ushered in the twenty-first century with the most uncommon of presidential elections. It had been 88 years since a minor-party candidate showed strongly enough to tip the election, and 112 years since the winner of the popular vote lost in the electoral college. That these events occurred together, in the same election in which the Supreme Court ultimately settled the contest, made it a rare political year indeed.

The 2000 election stands out for another reason also. It was the year in which campaigning through the Internet became de rigeur, opening up a new mode of candidate-voter interaction. Candidates had experimented with the Internet for several electoral cycles, going as far back as 1994, but the 2000 elections represented a leap forward by candidates in the degree of effort, money, and innovation dedicated to the Internet. In 1995, Representative Charlie Rose, Democrat from North Carolina, predicted that "by the year 2000 [the Internet] is going to be an indispensable campaign tool."[1] At least on the face of things, his prediction seemed correct as the races unfolded. For the major presidential candidates, the Internet became a component of the campaign rather than an afterthought, serving as a vehicle for targeted information dissemination, supporter reinforcement, volunteer recruitment and utilization, fundraising, and voter mobilization. In the Senate, three-quarters of the candidates used the Web to communicate their messages, up from just under half in 1996. In the House, 55 percent used the Web, up from only 16 percent in 1996.[2]

Not only were candidates nearly universally distributing their messages through the Internet, but their potential audience for on-line political communication had mushroomed. The 2000 elections were the first ever in which more than half of American adults were Internet users. And by 2000 these Internet users were spending significant amounts of time online. According to Nielsen ratings, the average time spent online from home was nearly ten hours per week, and when people went online, they spent an average of half an hour surfing the Web.[3] By 2000, Web users were more politically active than the general public, and they were more likely to vote. On the whole, surveys showed that roughly one-third of all Americans went online for political information, news, or other campaign-related activities in 2000.[4]

In politics no less than other realms of life, the Internet was on the American scene in 2000: Most candidates were using it, and a large and politically active fraction of citizens was involved. One of the lessons of American political history is that when a new medium is taken up by political candidates and voters alike, public expectations typically run high that democracy will be transformed for the better. In the 1830s and 1840s, for example, the new medium of the day was the mass newspaper. The so-called penny press arose overnight in historical terms, and it led to widespread expectations that citizens' capacity to follow the affairs of state would be dramatically improved. For the most part, these expectations eventually proved right. More than a century later, the introduction of television led to similar predictions. While television did lead to very large consequences for how campaigns are conducted and for the roles of voters, these were of a decidedly more mixed character.

What Then about the Internet?

Is this latest medium revolutionizing electoral politics? Are candidates centering their campaigns on Internet strategies? Are voters relying on it for electoral information? Are candidates' online messages affecting whether people become involved in the campaign and even how they vote?

There are reasons to believe the Internet may be having such an impact. The Internet differs substantially from what went before for a host of reasons. When television was new, a few media businesses operated a near-monopoly on political information. The three major broadcasting networks dominated television programming, and the lack of program alternatives had important political consequences. The famous Kennedy-Nixon debate in 1960, from which many date the birth of political television as a determinant of election outcomes, was important not just because John Kennedy looked better than Richard Nixon on television. The event mattered because for most Americans there were only three channels of television available, and all three carried the debate. At that moment, to watch television at all was to watch the same thing that every other viewer was seeing.

With modern information technology, including the rise of cable and satellite, those monopolies are weakening. Gone are the days when more than 90 percent of television sets were tuned to one of three networks and presidential speeches simultaneously preempted all televised programming.

While narrowcasting has evolved since the 1980s to be one aspect of contemporary television, it is one of the *defining* features of the Internet, where audience fragmentation and a multitude of sources and "broadcasters" are carried almost to their logical extreme. The number of Internet sites is in the tens of millions. A 2001 survey of Internet usage found that the top ten sites together attracted just under 17 percent of all Internet traffic.[5] Despite the undeniable clout of some key businesses in delivering content on the Internet, this is a far different media environment than when Kennedy and Nixon squared off on the three networks in 1960.

The interactive nature of the new media environment also makes it obviously different. Much is made of this term, largely for good reason. From the perspective of democracy, *interactive* does not merely mean that the Internet is somehow more engaging than television, like playing a game might be more interactive than looking at a painting. Interactive means that information flows in multiple directions. The fact that the Internet audience does not merely receive communication from candidates for office but reveals information and communicates outward makes the new medium potentially very different from traditional media.

Another characteristic that makes the Internet apparently different, at least from television, is that it is more purposive. To a very large degree online, what people see is the product of their choices and their intentional actions of typing or clicking. In the words of the U.S. Supreme Court, "[u]nlike communications received by radio or television, 'the receipt of information on the Internet requires a series of affirmative steps more deliberate and directed than merely turning a dial.' "[6] In the Court's application of the First Amendment to the Internet in the case of the Communications Decency Act, this fact made all the difference. How it might make a difference in other aspects of democracy, especially campaigns and elections, remains to be seen. But combined with other distinctions among new and old media, the purposiveness built into Internet use provides another reason to suspect consequences for politics.

Yet, these very features of narrowcasting, specialization, and choice also raise opposite questions. Does any particular political site draw such a narrow slice of the audience as to be irrelevant? Are the people who interact with a candidate's campaign site already supporters? If they are, what is the value to a campaign—let alone to democracy on a larger scale—of preaching to the converted? Could that be polarizing or harmful to political discourse? How can a specialized, purposive medium like the Internet compete with the power of television to attract and influence national audiences?

Speculation has been rampant about such matters by journalists, political professionals, and scholars. The debate is typified by two books published recently, both using the same trendy approach in their titles. In his book *Vote.com*, former Clinton consultant Dick Morris speculates that the Internet is improving democracy by informing citizens and undermining the power of political professionals and elites—

people like himself. With many others, Morris has bought into the idea that new technological capacities surely mean more engagement, better-informed citizens, and therefore improved politics. In *Republic.com*, law professor Cass Sunstein takes a less sanguine view. He hypothesizes that narrowcasting, specialization, and the purposiveness built into the Internet do little to overcome disengagement or citizens' lack of information about politics. Instead, he writes, the decentralizing, disintermediating effect of the Internet is potentially harmful to democracy because it contributes to fragmentation and divisiveness.[7]

What is conspicuously absent in these debates, which are now several years old, is systematic, scientifically collected data about the role of the Internet in elections. Taken together, the arguments of Morris, Sunstein, and others do little more than suggest many possible futures associated with new media and politics. What is desperately needed is hard evidence about who visits campaign Web sites and about how their experiences on the Internet affect them.

The purpose of this book is to present such evidence and to interpret what it tells us about the state of the Internet and campaigns for electoral office. We too bring a set of theoretical expectations to the table. These come from the study of past media and from the realm of political psychology. As we will argue later, these lead us to expect in advance that one side in the contemporary popular debate has the stronger hand. We present that case as a way of making sense of the many possibilities, and we aim to provide a variety of social scientific data that can advance the understanding of contemporary American campaigns.[8]

The Internet affords a unique chance to observe carefully a new medium at its inception. When mass newspapers broke on the political scene and some observers speculated that a development of historical proportions was at hand, for the most part that revolution went unrecorded from systematic perspectives.[9] Modern techniques of quantitative social science and polling did not arise until well into the twentieth century. Even when television emerged as a political medium in the 1950s and 1960s, few thought to examine its consequences for democracy until much later. Few political scientists took the role of television seriously as an object of study in the 1952 election, when television first emerged as a mass medium in political communications.[10] In contrast, this book is intended to help provide such a baseline for the Internet. American society in the early twenty-first century is at much the same stage with the Internet as it was with television in the mid-1950s. In 1950, television was in 9 percent of homes. By the end of that decade, 88 percent of homes possessed at least one television set.[11] The Internet is following a similar trajectory from single-digit reach in the mid-1990s to likely saturation by 2010. It is time to form a clearer understanding of what its future may hold.

Our Approach

The approach here is twofold, directed at how candidates use the Internet and at how citizens respond. We are interested in developing a portrait of the Internet and campaigns for democratic office from both sides, so to speak. On one side are the candidates who create and manage Internet-based campaign operations. We want to understand better the thinking and strategizing that goes into this process and the nature of the content that ends up in campaign Web sites. On the other side is the public, which forms their potential audience. We want to know who visits campaign Web sites, why, and what the consequences might be for them. We have therefore distilled the contemporary debate about the Internet and campaigning down into two main questions:

1. How do candidates present themselves online and how does that presentation compare with their use of traditional media?
2. What is the influence of Internet-based campaigns waged by candidates on voters' knowledge level, attitudes, and behavior (including voter turnout and vote choice)?

Our analysis of these questions is guided by two interrelated characteristics of campaign communications. One characteristic concerns the first question and has to do with the ways that candidates, journalists, and other political elites are able to direct the public's attention. We believe that understanding the effects of the Internet on politics requires evaluating how well candidates are able to direct the public's attention using "new" media.

The other characteristic, which relates to the second question, addresses voters' tendencies to filter political messages and to act with great selectivity as they navigate the political world. Understanding the effects of the Internet requires assessing how it influences voters' natural tendencies toward selectivity. These characteristics constitute our theoretical framework for thinking about the Internet in politics.

From this perspective, we sought to join together in this book two kinds of systematic evidence: an examination of the candidate side of campaigning on the Internet and an examination of the voter side. The study included the Web sites of the three major presidential campaigns of 2000 and two minor ones: George W. Bush, Al Gore, Ralph Nader, Pat Buchanan, and John Hagelin. It also included a state-level perspective, because state-level races possess a number of important differences from presidential contests. They often—though not always—involve candidates who are less well known, and they typically receive less coverage in the mass media. For reasons of cost, the project focused on just one carefully selected state. Conducting just one statewide survey is nearly as costly as conducting a national survey, and few researchers—ourselves included—are in a position to survey multiple states as well as the entire nation.

The state we chose is Missouri, the only state with races for both the Senate and governor that promised to be competitive in 2000. Missouri contains two metropolitan areas, suburbs, and a mix of rural and agricultural regions. Missourians also have a long record of voting for the presidential candidate who ends up winning nationwide, and all these factors made it the most typical state we could identify for the 2000 contest. In Missouri, we examined the U.S. Senate candidates, the gubernatorial candidates, and the candidates for secretary of state. These three races gave us a contrast between high and low media profile races.

For analyzing the candidate side of these races, the project involved interviews with campaign officials and content analyses of their Web sites. We archived the sites of candidates in these national and statewide races twice and then analyzed their content and strategy using a systematic approach to logging, or coding, how and what candidates said at their sites. Our telephone and in-person interviews with campaign staff took place during the races and soon after the November elections. Members of our research team spoke with campaign officials involved directly with Web sites from the major presidential campaigns—Bush, Gore, Nader, and Buchanan—and those working for Missouri candidates, including gubernatorial candidates Jim Talent and Bob Holden, U.S. Senate candidates Mel Carnahan and John Ashcroft, and the candidates for secretary of state, Matt Blunt and Steve Gaw. To provide perspective on the use of the Internet in the 2000 general election campaign, we also interviewed people who had been involved in Internet usage by candidates during the 2000 primaries and the 1998 elections, including some involved with the presidential campaigns of former senator Bill Bradley and Senator John McCain.

For the voter side of campaign communication, we conducted five randomized telephone surveys. Nationally, our surveys included a random sample of 1,000 adults, all of whom saw one of the major campaign sites in our study, which we call our Web audience survey, along with another random sample of 1,000 people who did not see a site, which we call our comparison survey. We conducted these telephone interviews mainly in October, during the heat of the campaign season. Following the election, we went back and reinterviewed two panels of 300 from among the Web audience survey. The fifth survey took place in the state of Missouri, where we collected a random sample of 500 people who had seen a presidential or state-level Web site under study.

As a complement to the surveys, the study also included laboratory experiments. These involved random samples of citizens in San Diego, St. Louis, Charlotte, and New York, who visited research facilities, filled out questionnaires, and then visited Web sites while in the experimental facility. When they were finished, they filled out follow-up questionnaires. About 200 people participated in this component of the study. The appendix of this book provides a lengthier discussion of how we went about the research.

The Internet has many dimensions, most of which are in flux. As of the year 2000, these included the Web, electronic mail, bulletin boards, chat rooms, and so on. In our research, we chose to focus on the Web, because it is an important locus of convergence among technologies and media. Radio, television, electronic mail, bulletin boards, chat rooms, and so on were by 2000 increasingly accessible through the Web. Within the Web, our focus on campaign sites meant setting aside other important categories: news sites sponsored by traditional media businesses, novel public affairs and discussion sites, Web logs sponsored by online businesses or other nontraditional sources, party Web sites, interest group Web sites, government Web sites, and individual sites.

Our rationale for doing so is straightforward and practical as well as theoretical. It is practical because candidate sites represent a smaller and more manageable pool of sites to analyze. It is theoretical because the purest form of candidate-voter communication is the one candidates initiate without filters. Only candidate Web sites allow the candidates complete control over the messages they send to voters.

These sites therefore constitute a key element of the larger Internet picture. We do not suggest that candidate-voter interaction at campaign Web sites is the same as other kinds of communication using new media or that it is necessarily representative of all aspects of politics. We do believe that what goes on at campaign Web sites is important in its own right and that a better understanding of campaign site dynamics can produce insights into how democracy may be changing and how it may be staying the same as media technology evolves.

The Evolution of Candidate Communication

The move by candidates onto the Internet during the 1990s represents the latest in a long series of changes in electoral communication that stretches far back in American history. Television is commonly cited as the key technological development that has affected how politics works. But the relationship between changes in technology and changes in politics encompasses far, far more than simply the broadcasting of images and sound. Since the time of the founding of the republic itself, technological developments have afforded candidates for office a stream of new techniques for communicating their messages. The rotary press, telegraph, railroad, radio, computerized direct mail, and other innovations each altered opportunities and costs for communicating political messages, and in each case parties and candidates responded.

During the early days of the United States, candidates campaigned for office by giving speeches around their districts. Sometimes opposing candidates would travel together to reduce expenses. They would arrive in a town, take turns speaking, and then spend the night in the same hotel room before traveling on to the next stop in the morning. The mental image of candidates like George Bush and Al Gore sharing a hotel room on the campaign trail strikes us now as ridiculously quaint, but the more important novelty of early candidates' actions was that they campaigned popularly at all. John Quincy Adams said of this practice: "One of the most remarkable peculiarities of the present time is that the principal leaders are traveling about . . . holding forth, like Methodist preachers, hour after hour, to assembled multitudes under the canopy of heaven."[1] In a time before mass media— before even the rise of the newspaper as a popular medium—the innovation of candidates for office communicating directly with the public at large can hardly be overstated.

Contrary to the idealized myth of the New England town meeting, which is notable as an exception rather than as the rule of democratic practices, politics in Adams's time was an elite affair, far removed from the everyday citizen. As communication scholar Michael Schudson shows, democratic norms at the time of the founding held that popular involvement in political decision making was a dangerous affair.[2] Decisions were best left to political nobles, for fear that the uninformed, illiterate citizenry would too easily be aroused to a mob mentality.

This legacy of political elitism from the founding eventually died away, setting in motion a democracy recognizable by modern standards for the first time. Property requirements for voting were abolished and popular elections for president spread among the states to direct the electoral college's decisions, which up through the 1820s were largely independent of popular voting by citizens. Those changes, along with other reforms, like the use of political conventions rather than closed-door caucuses to choose candidates, laid the groundwork for mass politics. In addition to political organizations, mass politics relied on the mass media for communication between candidates and voters.

Throughout the nineteenth century and well into the twentieth, political parties played powerful roles as party organizations recruited candidates, nominated them for office, raised and spent funds, and sponsored meetings, rallies, marches, speeches, and other events for citizens. They not only canvassed precincts on foot, rallying voters to the polls, but secured jobs for loyalists and helped new immigrants to find places in communities. Between the beginning of the Progressive

Era and the 1960s, these roles deteriorated. Simultaneously with and partly as an outgrowth of party organization decline, the use of television for campaigns grew. As it did, campaigning for office increasingly evolved into a process of large-scale communication, using mass media more than party-based organizing and mobilizing.[3] By the 1980s at least, American electoral politics had become a highly candidate-centered system, where voters placed less emphasis than before on party affiliation and more on the personal characteristics of a candidate conveyed through the media.[4]

Since the 1960s, television has been the prominent vehicle for presidential candidate communication both in terms of the amount of resources devoted to the medium and the number of voters reached by it. Television advertising constitutes the vast majority of a presidential candidate's advertising budget and a growing share of the total campaign budget. In 1992, the Clinton/Gore campaign spent 98 percent of its campaign advertising budget on television.[5] In 2000, the Gore camp spent 40 percent of its total federal campaign revenue on television advertising while the Bush campaign used 58 percent on television advertising.[6]

But television advertising alone is not effective in shaping voters' attitudes about candidates. Advertising is most effective when it reinforces impressions that voters have acquired from other sources, including news media coverage.[7] Therefore, candidates have learned that they must gain the attention of journalists in order to communicate with voters. This is particularly true of presidential candidates and their relationships with television network news reporters. Electoral campaigns devote large amounts of candidate time today to acquiring news media coverage, particularly favorable coverage, for their candidates. Candidates schedule news conferences, hold one-on-one interviews with journalists, meet with editorial boards, and issue press releases and news advisories to get the attention of the press. Campaigns arrange their candidates' public appearances to encourage news media attendance and, for many events, the primary purpose is to create a photo opportunity for the evening news. According to one presidential campaign staff member, "Everywhere we go, we're on a media trip. . . . we're attempting to generate as much free television and print, as much free radio, as we can get."[8]

As Judith S. Trent and Robert V. Friedenberg put it, "Communication is the means by which the campaign begins, proceeds, and concludes," while Edie N. Goldenberg and Michael W. Traugott posit that "conveying campaign messages to win votes is the central activity of political campaigns."[9] If democracy is about elections, elections are about communication, and so to understand how democracy works requires understanding how communication works and how it evolves over time.

Media Alternatives

By the early 1990s, candidates relied heavily on the traditional news media to get their messages out to voters. Yet, due to changes in the way news media covered campaigns, candidates increasingly were becoming frustrated with that level of dependence. Developments in the news business had resulted in a new approach to what constituted news. During the 1970s and 1980s, journalists gradually rejected the traditional concept of the reporter as simply a narrator of events. Increasingly, they saw their roles as interpreters of news events as well. Stories titled "news analysis" became more common features in newspapers. In those stories, the reporters gave themselves greater roles in describing and deciphering events, with less and less space or time offered to sources, including candidates, to explain themselves in their own words.

Candidates found their ability to speak directly to voters increasingly limited. One sign of this transformation of news was the *sound bite*—the amount of time that a candidate actually speaks on air in a broadcast news story. While in 1968 the average length of a sound bite was 42 seconds, by 1996 it had fallen to just over 8 seconds.[10]

Nor was the problem limited to television news. While in 1960 the front page of the *New York Times* averaged 14 quoted lines of the candidates' words, by 1992, this average had fallen to 6 lines.[11] Two communications scholars have concluded that "journalists have become more dominant, increasing their share of air time," and as a result "news casts have become more journalist-centered."[12]

The new role of the reporter led to charges that the news media were injecting their personal biases into their news stories. This bias was particularly directed at network evening news programs.[13] Republican candidates were particularly critical of the media as too sympathetic to Democrats. During the 1992 campaign, a widely circulated bumper sticker expressed this hostility toward the press. It read: "Annoy the Media. Re-elect Bush."

With the expansion of cable and satellite offerings, broadcast news found the serious political news audience migrating to more intensive news and information channels such as CNN or CNBC. Other news options also increased in number, such as feature news programs and entertainment news. Primetime soft news programs, such as *60 Minutes*, *20/20*, *Dateline*, and *48 Hours*, proliferated. They catered to consumers who were less interested in political news. The expansion of cable offerings even meant news programs were competing with entertainment programs for audience share, something unheard of in the heyday of television news dominance of the 1950s and 1960s, when the only viewing option at a certain early evening hour was the news.

All in all, the competition for the news audience was becoming sharper. Taking a marketing approach to news, newspapers surveyed their audiences to determine what audiences preferred to read in a newspaper. The result was a perception by news organizations that the audience had greater interest in news topics other than politics and government.[14] Accordingly, news organizations began to reduce their coverage of politics. Coverage of some particular areas of government, such as Congress and state government, suffered dramatically.[15]

Campaign coverage similarly was affected. In 2000, the three major networks spent a total of 805 minutes on presidential campaign coverage, despite the competitive nature of both the primary races and the general election campaign. During the last such competitive campaign (1992), network coverage was 1,400 minutes.[16]

In the general election, campaign coverage was only slightly greater on network television than it had been in 1996.[17] This is not good news when comparing the two elections since, in 1996, there was little suspense over who would be elected in November.

Even more disturbing for the candidates was the fact that when the campaign was covered, it did not mean the candidates actually had an opportunity to get their messages across. Instead, television coverage focused on the "horse race"—the current state of the competition among the candidates. Who was ahead and who was behind at the moment became more important than what the candidates stood for and what policies they proposed. More than seven of ten network television news stories in 2000 were about the horse race rather than other subjects, such as the candidates' records or policy positions.[18]

Perhaps another impetus for growing candidate dissatisfaction with the traditional news media was growing public disillusionment with news sources. For example, between 1993 and 2000, the percentage of Americans who expressed at least "quite a lot" of confidence in television news dropped from 46 percent to 36 percent.[19] By the end of the 1990s, Americans were more likely than ever before to characterize the press as immoral, unprofessional, and politically biased.[20]

By the 1990s, as traditional news forums became less accessible to candidates and as coverage turned away from policy issues that candidates sought to discuss, candidates' attention turned to other possible forums.[21] Simultaneously, the broadcast audience also found interest in new media forums. These new media are "mass communication forms with primarily non-political origins that have acquired political roles."[22] They include the media forums of talk radio, television talk programs, and television news magazines, among others.

Candidates gravitated to these forums because these media were less likely to filter their messages, and there was no expensive price tag as with paid political advertising. Candidates appeared on political talk radio shows featuring hosts such as Rush Limbaugh, Oliver North, and Michael Reagan. In addition, candidates found an even more sympathetic audience with many local or regional talk show hosts. Even controversial hosts attracted candidates to their shows. In 1992, Democratic presidential candidate Bill Clinton participated in Don Imus's *Imus in the Morning* program, as did Republican presidential candidate Bob Dole in 1996. In 1993, then New Jersey gubernatorial candidate Christine Todd Whitman made an appearance on the Howard Stern show.

Candidates also frequented television talk shows, including the morning news shows and the late-night programs, such as the *Tonight Show*, *Late Night with David Letterman*, and *Late Night with Conan*

O'Brien. Larry King Live also became a popular forum for presidential candidates. Ross Perot used the show in 1992 to announce he would accept a popular draft to run for president that year as an independent.

Television news magazines also featured in candidates' strategies to send messages to voters. In 1992, Bill and Hillary Clinton appeared on *60 Minutes* to discuss Gennifer Flowers's allegations of an extra-marital affair with the candidate. A few candidates also found MTV an attractive forum for reaching new voters. Bill Clinton even claimed that MTV "had a lot to do with the Clinton-Gore victory" in 1992.[23]

These new media forums attracted candidates for a number of reasons. One was the opportunity to communicate with voters without concern for a journalistic filter. Talk show hosts were not journalists, nor did they approach questioning candidates in the same way. They were less likely to pose gotcha-type questions. Questions often were of the softball variety, dealing with topics such as the candidates' personal interests and background. Another was the opportunity these venues provided candidates to present a more human portrait of themselves. Al Gore used the late-night shows to joke about his image as a wooden candidate and the powerlessness of his position as vice president. George W. Bush kissed Oprah Winfrey while appearing on her show.[24] But the jovial attitude of these sessions occasionally backfired on candidates. In March 2000, then-candidate Bush tastelessly joked about David Letterman's heart surgery.[25]

New media forums also gave candidates more time to develop answers to questions. With program lengths usually of two or three hours, talk radio hosts might allow a candidate a half hour or more. As a result, candidates were given the opportunity to develop less truncated answers. Not bound by the constraints of television news, candidates could expand on policy positions and offer rationales difficult to fit into ten-second television sound bites.

Launching Campaign Web Sites

The Internet as a political tool is best understood in this context of burgeoning alternatives to a traditional set of media with which so many were frustrated. It would not be quite right to say that candidates

19

for office as well as citizens took up the Internet *because* of the rising interest in media alternatives. Rather, the technologies of the public Internet became available simultaneously with the exploration of media alternatives under way for other reasons. The employment of various methods of campaign communication over time has been described as the evolution of campaigns from "premodern" through "postmodern."[26] The early use of political party communication networks and some reliance on print media characterized a premodern stage. The emergence of broadcast media, particularly television, signaled movement into modern campaigns. The most recent stage, termed the postmodern period, includes electronic networks, such as the Web and e-mail.

In the early 1990s, this new media forum—online communication—also gained public attention. Almost immediately the implications for candidates were probed and analyzed. The new medium quickly was viewed by political consultants, politicians, and journalists as one soon to become an essential tool in the hands of campaigns.[27] In 1994, one political activist predicted that "by 1996, we will begin to see some number of campaigns either won or lost because campaign operations either use or fail to use network communication and organization."[28]

Advantages of online communication quickly became obvious to many in the campaign industry, even if the idea of the Internet being decisive in a race was at best an unproven speculation. The Internet not only offered campaigns another avenue for reaching voters but was, in some respects, superior to offline communication forms. The costs of disseminating information to voters was minuscule compared to the amount devoted to television or print advertising. Initially, budgets for Web site creation and maintenance ran in the tens of thousands for presidential candidates, rather than the tens of millions needed for print and television advertising campaigns. One scholar estimated that "a month's tab for the Web could tally less than the [campaign] staff's monthly tab for donuts and coffee."[29]

Communication with the press also could be improved. News releases and press advisories could be mailed electronically, saving hundreds of dollars in the costs of faxes. Journalists would have a constant resource for information about the campaign, such as the texts of speeches, press endorsements, and notices of upcoming events. Since Web site information was available on demand, candidate information could be retrieved on the journalist's timetable, not just the campaign's.

Along with other forms of new media, these networks appeared ideal for unfiltered candidate communication. Candidates could devise their own messages and control the content of the presentations. The Web offered the opportunity to bypass journalists and speak directly to voters, while maintaining control of the message in the process. With the Web, the candidate could govern the production of the message: Web site layout and content were completely within the purview of the candidate. Although paid advertising also offered that level of control, the costs were exorbitant. Here was a low-cost medium that allowed the candidate to determine the content of the message received by the voter without worry over journalistic filtering. Other capacities of the Internet, such as facilitating the mobilization of volunteers and the channeling of donations, would become clear to campaign professionals later in the 1990s, but from this early perspective these advantages were not yet apparent.

Candidates quickly perceived, however, that this medium did not arrive without liabilities. First, the Internet plainly was less useful than, say, direct mail or newsletters because unlike those communication forms, the campaign lacked control over Web distribution.[30] Anyone could view a candidate Web site, including those who were not potential supporters and those who actually worked for the opposition. Like many interest groups, campaigns could password-protect their sites, but such a move might anger voters seeking information and incur criticism from the press about candidate secrecy.

Even more problematic was the size of the audience. Initially, the Internet audience was tiny compared to the total electorate. At the end of the 1980s, Internet usage was limited to a small number of academics and computer specialists. Even by the 1994 election, access to the Internet was available only to 3.5 million adults.[31]

Yet the limited audience problem was less acute than it seemed at first glance because of the nature of that potential audience for a candidate Web site. A look at the demographics of Internet users by the mid-1990s shows they tended to be registered voters who were at middle to high income levels and were fairly well educated—seemingly a model audience of potential voters.[32] One presidential candidate press secretary noted that the Internet "is a high-tech organization weapon with a potential national audience . . . of people who have a high propensity to vote."[33]

Even though Internet users were attractive to candidates for this reason, during the 1990s, the online campaign was not seen as more than a sideline to the traditional campaign. Nevertheless, a campaign Web site could not easily be dismissed. It became an increasingly essential campaign component, if for no other reason than to appeal to the niche of voters who were online and wanted to use the Web to gain information about candidates.

Development of a Web site meant including a new kind of staff—Web designers—which created fresh problems of integrating this new communication function into the campaign organizational chart. These individuals became known as campaign Webmasters. Yet, candidates and campaign managers accustomed to traditional media presentations were not sure how Webmasters fit into their organizations. How that integration occurred varied greatly depending on the campaign. The Webmaster's role became dependent on the understanding of the Internet by other campaign officials and whether campaigns were run hierarchically or laterally.

Typically, Webmasters were placed in the hierarchy under the director of communications. Yet, Webmasters sometimes needed more direct access to campaign managers and candidates, especially in situations where the communications director had little appreciation for the Internet's role and ignored the Webmaster. New organizational tension became a by-product of the inclusion of the Internet.

Despite the drawbacks, particularly in terms of audience size, campaigns increasingly developed Web sites and acquired e-mail addresses. Electronic candidate communication filtered down from presidential campaigns to statewide and then local races throughout the 1990s. From election year to election year, usage expanded and acquired increasing importance in campaign functions.

The first use of the Internet by a presidential candidate was undertaken by the Clinton campaign in the 1992 election. That year, the campaign placed campaign-related information, such as full texts of candidate speeches, advertisements, position papers, and biographical information about the candidates, on the Internet. But so few voters had Internet access at the time that the online information the campaign provided elicited only some curiosity from academics. There was little notice from journalists, and even less from voters, few of whom were aware of the Internet itself, much less a campaign's presence on it. The Bush campaign did not bother to respond with an online presence. The Clinton campaign's first step online led to the creation after the election of the first White House Web site and the administration's inclusion of the Web in its communication policies.[34] More candidates developed Web sites in the 1994 midterm races, but they were still few in number.

But early in the 1996 presidential campaign, following the introduction of the World Wide Web, with its graphic capabilities and commercial potential, experiments with the Internet in campaigns expanded. Republican presidential candidate Lamar Alexander was the first to utilize the Internet for campaigning when, during the primaries, he participated in interactive online sessions with users. Subsequently, other candidates developed campaign Web sites.

Supporters of potential candidates even created home pages to stimulate interest in prospective campaigns. Colin Powell was the subject of a Web site that urged him to run before he announced he would not do so. Supporters and opponents of announced candidates also developed their own Web sites. Bob Dole, Bill Clinton, and Pat Buchanan, among others, were the targets of attack sites. Some of these sites appeared, at first glance, to be the candidates' official sites, but on closer look were revealed as parody sites. One such site parodied the Pat Buchanan campaign in 1996 by mimicking the official Buchanan site's main page design. The parody site added subtle twists, such as the positioning of a small Nazi flag in the background.[35]

During one of the candidate debates, GOP presidential candidate Bob Dole announced the address for his World Wide Web home page

23

and encouraged voters to visit the site. Dole's act was an important milestone for the Internet as an election information tool since it showed a candidate using a traditional media forum to advertise his Web presence.

At this stage candidate Web sites merely reinforced campaign themes. Lamar Alexander emphasized his down-home roots by wearing a red plaid shirt while campaigning and taping television ads. Similarly, his Web site's main page was colored with red plaid. Bob Dole's site emphasized Dole's small-town beginnings and described one of the candidate's early jobs as a teenage drugstore soda jerk.

For the most part, candidate Web sites resembled brochures. This was not coincidental since many of the campaigns used the text and design of their brochures as the template for their campaign Web sites. There was little dynamic quality to the sites, which discouraged repeat visits for new information. For avid Internet users, this led to disappointment and frustration. "If [users] take a look at it and find something new, they're going to want to go back tomorrow or perhaps next week," explained one campaign Web site designer. "If they don't find something new, . . . not only are they discouraged, they feel that the candidate, or at least the Web site, wasted their time and resources by implying that there should be something."[36]

Eventually the campaigns began to conduct some experiments with online communication that went beyond "brochure-ware." The Clinton/Gore campaign invited site visitors to send electronic postcards to their friends. The Dole site offered campaign paraphernalia online.[37] Candidates also began utilizing e-mail as a means of communicating with voters. The Clinton/Gore campaign developed a general e-mail list with 5,000 names.[38] Such modest e-mail distribution lists in 1996 were not an effective get-out-the-vote tool, but they were a start.

Candidates were not the only purveyors of online campaign information. During 1996, a variety of election-related sites emerged. They represented political parties, interest groups, the news media, and nonprofit voter education organizations. National and local media outlets established their own Web sites, often with separate sections for election coverage.[39] Political parties developed their own sites at the national, state, and local levels. The two major party sites offered users dynamic graphics, clips of speeches, advertisements, press releases, convention speeches, and other party news. Minor party sites appeared as well. The Reform party, the Natural Law party, the Libertarian party, and the U.S. Taxpayers party all offered sites where voters could learn about each party's principles, news, and activities.

Yet only candidate sites offered the direct, unfiltered communication to voters for which candidates had been searching. With the proliferation of sites by 1996, candidates for all offices began to feel they needed some kind of exposure to the Web to appear competitive and up-to-date. Traditional media did much to reinforce this view. *Campaigns & Elections*, the publication for the elections industry, carried a series of articles about candidate use of the Web.[40] Newspaper stories proliferated about candidates' use of the Web to reach voters. At the end of the campaign, the *Wall Street Journal* even published lists of the best and the worst sites. Web addresses appeared in campaign literature, in media advertisements, and even on billboards and lawn signs. Two scholars concluded after 1996 that, though the Internet "has not fully arrived as a means of campaign communication, it certainly has a foot in the door."[41]

1998 Elections

The 1998 midterm elections turned the attention of nonpresidential candidates to Internet use. Congressional candidates' presence on the Web had been minimal in 1996. That year, only a minority of federal candidates had Web sites. A majority of major-party senatorial candidates and more than four out of five major-party House candidates did not have Web sites.[42]

By 1998, however, Internet use by statewide and congressional candidates was widespread. According to one survey, more than seven of ten major-party candidates for the U.S. Senate had campaign Web sites, as did 95 percent of major-party candidates for governor. More than one-third of major-party congressional candidates also posted campaign Web sites.[43] Still, use of Internet sites by candidates for local office continued to be rare.[44]

Internet use was most widespread in competitive races. All major-party candidates for the U.S. Senate in competitive races had Web sites, as did 57 percent of major-party U.S. House candidates in competitive races.[45] Internet presence was even more common in U.S. House open seats, where 64 percent of candidates in those races posted Web sites.[46]

The best-known use of the Internet during an election was the successful candidacy of former professional wrestler Jesse Ventura, who won 37 percent of the vote and the governorship of the state of Minnesota. Ventura's campaign suffered from a shortage of money, particularly compared with the well-funded Democratic and Republican candidates, both of whom were well-known political leaders in the state. Ventura raised $50,000 of his $600,000 campaign treasury from the Internet. More important, the Ventura campaign used the Internet extensively to answer charges by opponents or the news media, to update supporters on the activity of the campaign, and to mobilize supporters. He also developed an extensive e-mail list, which was used for recruiting volunteers and mobilizing voters on election day.[47]

The argument that the Internet would level the playing field for minor-party candidates had been made several years earlier. One scholar had predicted that "cyberspace campaigning might well facilitate the growth of minor parties and independent candidates who are currently largely priced out of extensive campaigning."[48] Two others suggested that "in the future the political system may no longer be dominated by the Democratic and Republican parties."[49] Now, the experience of the Jesse Ventura candidacy seemed to provide clear evidence that the Internet was offering a new opportunity for minor parties.

But the Ventura experience was the exception, not the rule. Overall, the test failed. In 1998, only one-third of independent or minor-party candidates for the U.S. Senate or Congress even posted Web pages.[50] None won election to statewide office or Congress, with the exception of Ventura and Representative Bernie Sanders of Vermont, a long-time incumbent.

A major drawback for minor-party, independent, or other resource-poor candidates was the growing financial cost of a Web presence.[51] More sophisticated sites with higher production values, interactivity, and changing content cost increasingly large sums of money. By 1998, the idea from the earlier elections—that anyone could afford a Web site—was changing. It was still true that anyone could afford at least a nominal site, but a really good Web site was beyond some candidates' reach. One survey by *Campaigns & Elections* found that 86 percent of campaigns with million-dollar budgets had Web sites, but just over one-half of those with budgets of $50,000 or less posted Web sites.[52]

Despite growing use of the Internet, campaigns were reluctant to devote large sums to electronic campaigning. *Campaigns & Elections* found that 80 percent of surveyed campaigns intended to spend less than $2,000 on designing and maintaining Web sites, and more than half of those said they would devote less than $500.[53] One campaign manager admitted that he would not spend much on a Web site because "I don't know what it's worth."[54] By 1998, the Internet was a political bandwagon, but many were unsure it had any impact on voters.

Some features of the Internet, such as interactivity or specialized information, were still underutilized in campaigns. Web sites still looked like electronic brochures.[55] Interactivity was more illusion than reality as site visitors could send messages to campaigns via e-mail, but responses were rare. According to one study, while 72 percent of campaign Web sites allowed visitors to answer a questionnaire or post an e-mail message, only two sites actually featured responses by the candidates.[56]

Still other functions also remained largely untapped. Nearly one-half of congressional sites failed to use them for fundraising or volunteer solicitation. However, fundraising was more common (over 70 percent) among competitive races, such as U.S. Senate races and U.S. House campaigns for open seats.[57] The vast majority of those using the Web for volunteer solicitation recruited help for traditional volunteer activities, not online roles. Even providing simple voter registration information was neglected by nearly nine of ten congressional candidate sites.[58]

But campaigns did discover e-mail, although it was used primarily for internal purposes, such as communication with fellow staffers or volunteers. One survey of 1998 campaigns concluded that e-mail "is seen by most campaigns more as a tool of internal communications and organizational mobilization as opposed to a vehicle for voter persuasion."[59] One well-publicized exception was the Ventura campaign that year. Ventura's gubernatorial campaign used e-mails to its supporters across the state to notify them of upcoming candidate rallies. The list, which included approximately 3,000 e-mail addresses, was called JesseNet and became an inexpensive way for a poorly funded candidate to communicate with and mobilize supporters.[60]

The 1998 electoral cycle showed expanding usage of the Internet by candidates, but what was lacking was evidence that such usage made any difference in the electoral outcome. In fact, according to one study of candidate use of the Web, there was "little difference in Internet campaigning between winners and losers."[61] Nevertheless, campaigns, particularly those with serious competition, began to see the potential of the Internet for internal campaign functions such as the management of data and internal campaign communication.[62]

2000: The Year of the Internet

As presidential election years go, the campaigns in 2000 had unusual characteristics. Control of both the House and Senate was up for grabs, and the presidential polling numbers showed a very close race for the White House after the second convention. Following the Bush campaign's announcement of Dick Cheney as running mate in July, the polls showed Bush with a six-point lead, which widened slightly following the Republican convention in August.[63] The numbers changed following the September Democratic convention, with Gore drawing roughly even with Bush in the mid-40 percent range. The polls continued to show a dead heat until election day.[64]

In Congress, the situation was similar. Republicans had only a five-seat majority in the Senate, and a change of five or six seats in the House would give the chamber to the Democrats. With the White House, the Senate, and the House all closely contested for the first time in decades, the stakes in 2000 were high. Indeed, Republicans would retain the House and win control of the Senate with 50 seats plus Dick Cheney's tie-breaking vote as vice president, but then lose

Senate control in 2001 with the defection of Vermont Republican senator Jim Jeffords.

Less unusual but still atypical was the strong challenge by Ralph Nader as a minor-party candidate. With the contest between Gore and Bush clearly a tight one, the strong likelihood that Nader votes would come disproportionately from the Gore column gave the election a meaningful three-way dynamic, even though Nader had little chance of taking even one state, let alone winning office.

Concern by Democrats about Nader's effect would prove well founded. A Gallup poll about a week before the election showed about 40 percent of Nader voters reporting they would vote for Gore if Nader were not in the race, while 20 percent said they would vote for Bush.[65] A USA Today poll of Nader supporters put the figures at 43 percent for Gore, 21 percent for Bush, 21 percent saying they would abstain from voting if Nader were not running, and the remainder undecided.[66]

While it is clear that Gore enjoyed a substantial and consistent advantage over Bush among Nader supporters nationally, we do not know exactly how Nader voters would have behaved on a state-by-state basis if their candidate were not in the race, which is the key question in assessing whether Nader's presence gave the election to Bush. But if the state-level figures in Florida, as well as a few other key states, even roughly approximated the aggregate national figures, then Nader's presence in the race did tip the election to Bush.

Viable primary challenges to Bush and to Gore up until New Hampshire were also an important feature of the campaign season. Polls showed Democratic challenger Bill Bradley running roughly even with Vice President Gore throughout most of the fall of 1999, with a lead for a while in New Hampshire. The poll figures, combined with comparable levels of fundraising by Bradley, made his campaign a serious challenge to Gore, at least for a while. However, a television advertising blitz by Gore in that state in the month before the campaign eroded the Bradley challenge and contributed to Gore's 52 percent to 47 percent win there.[67]

In the Republican race, John McCain played Bradley's role. Though poll numbers showed McCain well behind George Bush and though a large disparity in fundraising existed, McCain's upset of Bush in New Hampshire (49 percent to 31 percent) gave McCain a huge if short-lived boost. McCain then contested South Carolina heavily with much of his remaining funding.[68] His loss there, at the end of his financial rope, effectively ended his campaign.

In the general election, the central features of Bush's strategy in 2000 included education and tax policy proposals, a focus on character by attempting to associate Gore with Clinton, and an effort to attract minority voters by emphasizing urban educational failures. The tax cut was the centerpiece of Bush's policy initiatives, dominating both his televised advertisements and his debate rhetoric.[69] It served both as a broadly popular lure to taxpayers and as a vehicle for appealing to conservatives with a message of reducing the size of government. Education reform similarly tapped into an issue of broad public concern and provided a means for Bush to attempt to convince African-American voters that he was concerned with the plight of inner cities.

Gore's strategy prior to the convention reflected his trailing status and shifted somewhat as he drew even. His "Progress and Prosperity" tour promised a continuation of the economic boom, retirement of the debt, protection for Social Security, and expanding prosperity to all citizens. Following the convention, his focus shifted toward an emphasis on the political center and a deemphasis of party differences, though he continued to address the environment and issues involving race.[70]

Both Gore and Bush focused their campaign advertising in ways that are relevant to long-term trends in technology and media. Both emphasized targeted advertising crafted to convey specific messages to particular media markets. Rather than running nationwide advertisements on the networks, as had happened in the previous two presidential elections, Bush and Gore addressed themselves to local television audiences, making appeals and counterappeals that often revolved around quite narrow issues, such as prescription drug benefits.[71] Bush even ran "instant ads" developed and broadcast on a daily or near-daily cycle. Darrell West calculates that about 60 percent of advertisements by the two campaigns focused on domestic policy issues and 31 percent on the personal qualities of the candidates, generally continuing the trend of emphasizing personality that had been growing stronger since the mid-1980s.[72]

The Missouri Races in 2000

The situation in Missouri, our state-level focus in this book, was as competitive and nearly as surprising as the national-level scene. The race for the U.S. Senate represented a clash of titans: the sitting governor challenging a senator for his seat. Both candidates, Senator John Ashcroft and Governor Mel Carnahan, were perennially popular Missouri politicians; both already had won several statewide races. Ashcroft even harbored national ambitions and had been rumored as a prospective presidential candidate in 2000 before committing to run for reelection to his Senate seat instead. Ashcroft, who had been elected to the Senate in 1994 after two terms as Missouri's governor and two as the state's attorney general, was a staunch conservative, supporting school vouchers, fewer restrictions on gun ownership, privatization of Social Security, and an end to affirmative action. The one-term senator also held a reputation as a strong moralist who hailed from the Bible Belt of southern Missouri. He presided over prayer meetings in his Senate office and was a devout churchgoer. Not surprisingly, Ashcroft was an early advocate of President Clinton's resignation over the Monica Lewinsky affair.

As the 2000 election approached, leaders of the religious right had sought out Ashcroft for a possible presidential bid. He was particularly attractive because of his record of strong conservative religious views and his unwavering support of policy proposals such as constitutional amendments in support of school prayer and against abortion. Their overtures to Ashcroft ultimately failed, and the religious right was left with less-attractive alternatives. The three candidates who emerged from the religious right—Steve Forbes, Gary Bauer, and Alan Keyes—all performed poorly in GOP primary contests.

When Ashcroft bowed out of the presidential race, he returned to what seemed like a straightforward, if not easy, bid for reelection. Missouri's senior senator, Kit Bond, also a former governor and a moderate Republican, typically had coasted to victory. Unlike Bond, Ashcroft had carved out a niche in the right wing of the Republican party and therefore had attracted significant opposition from Democrats. They were elated when their best possible candidate, the incumbent governor, decided to take on the junior senator.

Carnahan also was no stranger to Missouri politics, a family tradition for him. His father had served seven terms as a U.S. representative from Missouri, and the future governor had spent his formative years in Washington, D.C., while his father served in Congress. Carnahan was from the small town of Birch Tree in south-central Missouri. He graduated from George Washington University, served a stint in the Air Force, and then later graduated from the law school at the University of Missouri.

Carnahan's first political office was in the Missouri House of Representatives. Then, after a defeat for the state senate, he practiced law for several years before returning to politics to make a successful run for state treasurer in 1980. Carnahan served as the state's treasurer for four years, lost a bid for the Democratic gubernatorial nomination, and then won election as lieutenant governor in 1988. He then served as lieutenant governor (while Ashcroft was governor) for four years. Carnahan was elected to succeed Ashcroft in 1992 and, like Ashcroft, by 2000 had served two terms as governor.

Since Missouri governors are term limited, Carnahan faced a withdrawal from politics in January 2001. Instead, he decided to vie for Ashcroft's seat. At that time, Ashcroft was sending signals that he would not run for reelection but would instead launch a bid for the presidency. When Ashcroft finally decided against a presidential bid in favor of reelection, the scene was set for a major clash between two enormously successful political figures.

Carnahan was known as a moderate Democrat in the mold of the centrist arm of the Democratic party, yet his candidacy offered a stark contrast with Ashcroft's positions on key issues such as abortion, the death penalty, gun owners' rights, and health care. His popularity as governor guaranteed a close race. Carnahan possessed more resources than most Senate challengers. He had high name recognition, strong favorability ratings, and sufficient financial support to face Ashcroft. Both national party organizations realized that the outcome of the Missouri race could determine party control of the U.S. Senate. By mid-October, the two candidates were neck and neck in the polls.

However, on the night of October 16, Carnahan, his son, and a campaign advisor were killed in a plane crash on the way to a campaign event. The tragedy stunned Missourians. Senator Ashcroft promptly suspended his campaign for a week. Organizers considered canceling the presidential candidate debate scheduled for October 17 in St. Louis, but eventually continued with the event. Remarkably, Carnahan was not the first major U.S. Senate candidate in Missouri to die in a plane crash. In 1976, Representative Jerry Litton, who had just that day won the Democratic party nomination for the U.S. Senate, was killed in a crash near Chillicothe, Missouri. Democratic party leaders chose former governor Warren Hearnes to replace Litton on the ticket. Hearnes subsequently lost to Ralston Purina executive and former minister John Danforth, who served for 18 years before being succeeded by John Ashcroft.

Governor Carnahan's death meant state Democrats had no viable candidate against John Ashcroft. Even potentially worse, according to Missouri election laws, it was too late for Carnahan's name to be removed from the ballot. Voters would have to choose between Ashcroft and his deceased opponent, or Democrats could offer a substitute who would agree to serve out the term if Carnahan were elected. The governor's widow, Jean Carnahan, was the logical candidate, and shortly after Lieutenant Governor Roger Wilson became acting governor for the remainder of Carnahan's term, which would end in January 2001, he ratcheted up the pressure on Mrs. Carnahan. Without a public commitment from her, Wilson announced he would appoint Mrs. Carnahan, if Missouri voters elected her late husband to the seat. Just eight days before the election, Jean Carnahan acknowledged she would accept appointment to the U.S. Senate if Mel Carnahan won the election.

The Carnahan campaign created a last-minute drive to maintain support for the Democratic candidate. Mrs. Carnahan taped a simple message to Missouri voters, which appeared as a television ad in the final days before the election. Buttons reading "I'm Still for Mel" were sent to 750,000 Missouri households.[73] And a last-minute Web site was created to support Jean Carnahan. Throughout this period, the Ashcroft campaign faced an unwelcome dilemma: How do you run a campaign against a dead man? Ashcroft himself at one point remarked: "I don't know who my opponent is, or if I have an opponent."[74] While Republicans initially may have concluded that Missouri voters would not elect a dead man, compassion for the late governor and the agreement of his widow to serve in his place offered Democrats new hope. In addition, no woman had ever served as a U.S. senator from Missouri. The candidacy of Jean Carnahan offered a new wrinkle to the campaign as a historical novelty but also offered a new appeal to women voters.

On election day, Senator Ashcroft enjoyed the unenviable distinction of losing an election to a dead opponent. He lost by 49,000 votes out of more than 2 million cast. Ashcroft was stoic in accepting the results and discouraged Republican party attempts to challenge the electoral outcome or the appointment of Jean Carnahan. While in November 2000 he seemed to be retired from politics, by late December he had gained an even higher profile role when he was tapped to be attorney general in the new Bush administration. After the terrorist events of September 11, 2001, Ashcroft acquired even greater responsibility. Meanwhile, Jean Carnahan was appointed to fill the Senate seat her husband had won posthumously.

The governor's race in Missouri lacked this kind of drama but was important nonetheless. In company with only nine other states, Missouri elects its governor in presidential election years. With no incumbent in the governor's race, the competition promised to be intense, the campaigns interesting, and the outcome close. Coming into the general election campaign, both parties believed they could win the governor's office. Polls at the time of the August primary indicated that the two major-party candidates were neck and neck.

The candidates both had established records. Democrat Bob Holden had been the state's treasurer for two terms after serving three terms in the Missouri House of Representatives. Holden also had unusual voter appeal. He was from the southwestern part of the state, a section where Democrats do less well and that is also the home region of John Ashcroft. Yet, Republican Jim Talent also had his own strength in a traditional Democratic area. Hailing from Chesterfield, a suburb of St. Louis, Talent had served as a member of Congress for eight years, following a stint as the minority leader in the Missouri House of Representatives.

Despite the intensity of the race, the campaign attracted only a moderate amount of media coverage during the election year. One campaign story six months before the election commented on the lack of news coverage:

> If Regis Philbin wants to eliminate contestants on his hit game show, he might consider asking this question: Who's running for governor this year in Missouri?
>
> It even stumps a lot of Missourians, if Wednesday's noontime sampling of downtown workers is any indication.
>
> Nobody could name the two major contenders: Republican Jim Talent, a congressman from Chesterfield, and Democrat Bob Holden, Missouri's state treasurer.[75]

The governor's race was overshadowed by the higher-profile U.S. Senate race between two powerhouses in Missouri politics. One candidate's campaign manager admitted as much: "We're definitely not a marquee race in the minds of voters."[76] In fact, both candidates even tied their campaigns to the respective Senate candidates. Holden vowed to continue the work of Governor Mel Carnahan, a promise that became more poignant after Carnahan's sudden death. Talent campaigned with John Ashcroft to lean on the senator's popularity.

The lower profile of the race also can be attributed to the two candidates' personal campaign styles. Neither was known for aggressive campaigning. Jim Talent acknowledged that the gubernatorial campaign was intentionally devoid of fireworks: "I don't believe in [personal attacks]. It's not my style, and I probably wouldn't be good at it. . . . I think the campaign [on both sides] was a little higher brow, and I don't think it hurt either of us. So I think there's a lesson there."[77]

Both candidates emphasized education, health care, and highway construction in public debates, speeches, and television ad campaigns. Although they differed on significant issues and sought to illuminate those differences in television ads, the campaign remained secondary in the public's attention to the drama of the Senate campaign before October 16, but even more so afterward.

On election day, Bob Holden barely emerged as the victor, winning by a mere 29,000 votes out of more than 2 million cast. Two years later, Jim Talent challenged Jean Carnahan for the U.S. Senate and won.

The race for the office of secretary of state fell well below most voters' radar. The two major-party candidates were unknown to most Missouri voters. Democrat Steve Gaw was the speaker of the Missouri House of Representatives and a former city prosecutor in the north-central Missouri town of Moberly. Republican Matt Blunt, a state legislator from Springfield, was the son of a member of Congress, Roy Blunt, who previously had served as secretary of state. Neither candidate had run a statewide campaign, but both had reputations as political comers. Blunt had barely served one term as a state legislator and was not yet 30, while Gaw was a veteran legislator and had served four years as speaker of the Missouri House even though he was only 43.

The race heated up slightly in the waning days of the campaign as the candidates engaged in negative television advertising campaigns. The two candidates exchanged barbs over their legislative records. Yet traditional media coverage was light. The *St. Louis Post-Dispatch*, the largest circulation newspaper in the state, published only three articles about the race between the primary and general election. Two of the three were about the charges the candidates hurled at each other in their television ads. Only one article provided background about the candidates. If ever there was a low-salience, low-information statewide campaign, this was it.

It proved to be another tight contest, and on election night Matt Blunt won by just 43,000 votes, bucking the tide of victorious statewide Democratic candidates. Gaw's last-minute negative ad campaign attacking Blunt's support of a legislative bill may have backfired, particularly since the *St. Louis Post-Dispatch* called the ad "misleading and inaccurate."[78]

This then was the political context for the campaigns' efforts to reach the public through the Internet in 2000. Perhaps the two most important aspects of this context were the competitiveness of so many races and the highly variable levels of public awareness and media attention. Especially as the general campaign season wore on and it became increasingly clear that outcomes would be close, the campaigns adopted the view that every little bit helps. The 1998 election had been viewed as an opportunity lost as candidates underutilized the new medium for campaigning.[79] Some had expected the 2000 election to finally be the "Year of the Internet" in electoral politics, while others saw 2000 as merely another step in the direction of a new kind of politics still several election cycles away. Dal Col, Forbes's campaign manager, envisaged: "In time, the whole political communications process will be based on the Web."[80] David C. King predicted:

> The Web coordinator of tomorrow's campaigns will be at the heart of any election strategy because the Web will soon be a device for collecting information about issues and specific individuals likely to support one's candidate, for "narrowcasting" about policies that concern voters most, and for helping campaign volunteers feel more a part of the campaign organization.[81]

If there ever were to be a year where the Internet might play the role that television apparently did in 1960, 2000 appeared to be it. The presidential race was close and featured a minor-party candidate with the potential to sway the outcome. The Senate was up for grabs and featured many close races also, like the Ashcroft-Carnahan battle in Missouri. Others, like the Talent-Holden contest, were almost invisible in traditional media. Any factor that might influence a few votes one way or the other could reasonably be considered politically important, and the Internet appeared to qualify. While in 1996 the online user audience had been small, it had grown considerably over the intervening years. In 1996, about one of four American adults was online.[82] By the winter of 2000, more than half of all Americans were online.[83]

The 2000 Presidential Primaries on the Internet

Early moves on the Internet by presidential candidates seemed to confirm that the precampaign speculation about the Internet's electoral role was prescient. Steve Forbes became the first presidential candidate to announce his candidacy through this medium. The Forbes site reminded visitors of the new ground the candidate was breaking when it proclaimed: "You and I are entering the information age—and the Washington politicians are stuck in the Stone Age."[84]

Candidates for offices from president to county commissioner posted Web sites throughout the year, far exceeding the number of candidate sites in 1998. As we have previously stated, by November 7, most major-party candidates for Congress had Web sites, and many other statewide and local candidates also created Web presences for themselves.

Many state and county election officials placed candidate and election information online for the first time. In some states, they included URL links or e-mail addresses to facilitate access to online candidate information, to the campaign, or even to the candidate.

Even more important potentially than mere presence online, candidates were integrating their online efforts into traditional campaign efforts. The online presentation of the candidate became more than an afterthought or an online brochure, as had been true in earlier elections. Al Gore's primary site featured a section where visitors could pose questions to the campaign. Steve Forbes's staff carried around digital cameras and satellite transmitters so feeds could be uploaded to the Internet site.[85] Not only did more candidate Web sites exist, but they connected to numerous facets of the campaigns, including fundraising, volunteer solicitation, voter reinforcement, and voter mobilization.

Thanks to a Federal Election Commission ruling in 1999, for the first time in an electoral campaign, candidates were authorized to raise money online and receive matching funds for those donations. The policy was initiated when the Bill Bradley campaign asked for matching funds from online donations.[86] A few candidates in nonpresidential races had taken credit card donations online in 1998, but the FEC ruling offered an incentive to presidential candidates to boost their online solicitation efforts. Not only could candidates solicit funds online, but they could attract e-mail recipients to the site to do so.

Presidential candidates quickly began incorporating online donations capabilities into their Web sites. Early reports suggested that the change would be lucrative for candidates. As early as the fall of 1999, the Bill Bradley campaign site already had raised more than $600,000 from 3,700 donors while the John McCain campaign had netted $260,000.[87] The Bush campaign eventually averaged $200,000 to $300,000 after each e-mailing.

But the most dramatic Internet fundraising story occurred in the wake of the New Hampshire primary. After McCain's surprise upset victory there on February 2, his campaign reported receiving $1.4 million in online contributions over a three-day period.[88] At the peak of this giving frenzy, online contributions were registering at the rate of $18,000 per hour.[89]

That rapid an increase in Internet fundraising was not matched during the rest of the primary season (nor in the general election).[90] The Gore campaign estimated it raised approximately $2.7 million over the entire primary season, while the Bush campaign reported getting $1.6 million via online donations.[91]

The McCain windfall was a product of the newness of the candidate's appeal as well as intensive traditional media coverage. The saturation coverage of McCain's New Hampshire primary win resulted in new interest, donations, and volunteers to the campaign in whatever way people could contact it. It was probably not the Internet itself that created interest in his campaign because this phenomenon had occurred before, even without the Internet. Previous underdog winners of the New Hampshire primary, such as Gary Hart (1984), Paul Tsongas (1992), and Pat Buchanan (1996), acquired similar unexpected boosts in their campaigns.

The difference was in the speed with which the candidate could profit financially from his new momentum. Unlike previous cases of sudden victory and media saturation, McCain was able to reap the benefits of his media windfall much more quickly since donations flooded in over a period of hours rather than days or weeks. The campaign then successfully turned the donations into more media advertising.

The McCain team also was creative in how it integrated fundraising and the Internet. For example, the campaign invited Internet users to chat with John McCain online, but only if they donated $100 to the campaign first. Five hundred people did so.[92]

The volunteer identification and solicitation effort also reached new heights. The Forbes campaign claimed to have signed up 30,000 online volunteers.[93] According to the Bradley campaign, 12 percent of the visitors to the Bradley Web site volunteered to assist the candidate.[94]

Online volunteer solicitation was designed to integrate site visitors into the work of the campaign. One experience related by Lynn Reed of the Bradley campaign demonstrates how a primary campaign used its e-mail list to identify volunteers to participate in canvassing neighborhoods:

> In the summer, we decided to canvass in New Hampshire. That was really early [in the campaign season]. So we e-mailed about 5,000 people who were within driving distance. . . . About 300 replied, and of those, about two-thirds showed up. We could never have afforded to make the phone calls with that rate of return. But this didn't cost us anything.[95]

For the most part, the campaigns had learned from earlier online efforts that many Web site visitors preferred online activism rather than the traditional campaign activities of licking envelopes or placing literature on doorknobs. As a consequence, online volunteer forms, common in previous elections, were supplemented by online tool kits. These were pages where site visitors could get instructions and assistance with writing letters to editors, organizing their neighborhoods, raising money, and so on, without ever meeting a campaign staffer or seeing a bricks-and-mortar campaign office.

Other ways that candidates sought to move their supporters toward online activism on their behalf included Vice President Gore's campaign home page, which encouraged visitors to become online field organizers responsible for sending e-mail to their friends. Republican candidate Steve Forbes urged supporters to sign up their friends on Forbes's e-mail distribution list. Forbes's supporters could create an "e-block" with as few as 12 other people. When they subscribed 5,000 other people, supporters became members of Forbes's National E-Committee.

During the primary season, the presidential campaigns used e-mail to spread news and reinforce voters. The goal was to create as large an e-mail list as possible. As examples, the Bradley camp claimed to have 85,000 names by the end of the campaign; the Bush campaign said it had 120,000.[96] But secondary to that was the need to obtain information about the people whose names were on those lists. E-mail lists, like direct mail lists, worked best if they could be targeted. Campaigns began to couple a basic e-mail address with information about the voters, particularly when it involved location.

A key problem was how to acquire e-mail addresses from site visitors. Although candidates could purchase lists of e-mail addresses, they learned that unsolicited e-mails had the potential to go awry. In one primary campaign in Georgia in 1998, a candidate had to apologize for sending a spam (unsolicited e-mail) message to voters. The candidate also lost the race.[97]

One method for getting e-mail addresses was to encourage site visitors to sign up for e-mail announcement lists. Another was to circulate sign-up lists at events. Still another was to encourage supporters to refer their friends and associates to the campaign.

Once e-mail lists were created, then the question arose as to how often to make contact with the subscribers. Some campaigns were much too intrusive—sending several e-mail messages daily and turning off potential supporters who did not want their e-mail boxes inundated with campaign propaganda, even for candidates they supported. Some candidates began to offer potential e-mail subscribers choices about frequency of contact with the campaign.

Candidates also sought to reinforce supporters by making themselves available to chat with site visitors. Vice President Al Gore's Web site featured real-time interactive town hall meetings where the candidate occasionally logged on to chat with participants. Other campaign discussion forums facilitated supporters talking to each other. Republican candidate Pat Buchanan's site featured visitor access to Buchanan chat rooms and message boards.

Encouraged by the campaigns, e-mail lists also were formed by supporters. These unofficial lists helped other candidate backers stay informed about campaign news and jointly discuss the candidate's campaign.

For the first time, many campaigns emphasized mobilization via electronic communication. For example, in order to encourage caucus participation in Iowa, the Bradley campaign created a separate Web site—www.caucusforbradley.com—and, through television ads, drove Internet users to the site. According to the campaign, through that site in the week before the Iowa caucus, 800 previously unknown supporters were identified.[98]

Moving into the 2000 General Election on the Internet

Clearly, by the 2000 primaries, online communication constituted a new tool for information dissemination and exchange, far beyond the electronic brochure of most earlier campaigns. One of the surest signs that the Internet had arrived on the American electoral scene was its role in political skirmishes for the first time. The Bush campaign challenged a parody site appearing in May 1999, claiming in a complaint to the Federal Election Commission that the site violated FEC rules. Even the candidate entered the fray by saying that "there ought to be limits" to the freedom to criticize on the Internet and called the site creator a "garbage man." In the minds of the Bush camp as well as the media, the Internet was a significant part of the world of campaigning. But the penalty would go to Bush, who was criticized by the press and some Internet users for seeking to stifle free speech.[99]

In describing his own Web site, Steve Forbes's Webmaster summarized the state of the Internet by 2000: "We're not just posting a Web page, we're launching a huge communications network for current and prospective Forbes supporters."[100] These new networks included not only the campaign's own staffers and volunteers but also much broader groups of supporters around the country who, in turn, created their own cybernetworks encompassing family, friends, or acquaintances with whom they communicated about the campaign.

In the next chapter, we will take a closer look at how the candidates used the Internet to build and support those networks—what strategies they employed, what audiences they addressed, and how they presented themselves.

42

Candidate Approaches to Election Web Sites

Does the Internet gain us votes? What is the best way to use the new capacities that the Internet provides? These questions were central to the campaigns in 2000, even as they committed many hundreds of thousands of dollars to developing and extending their Internet operations throughout the general election season.

These questions reflect an uncertainty on the part of candidate campaigns about how effective this new medium would be in helping secure electoral victory. Using content analyses and interviews with the staff associated with candidate campaigns, this chapter will look at how the various organizations attempted to answer these questions in the 2000 campaign. (For a discussion of our methodology, see the appendix.) We will examine candidate strategies and goals and how these were reflected in the content and functions built into their Web sites.

The Internet is not simply plopped into an electoral campaign. Rather, to reach voters, candidates adopt strategies that address various aspects of the campaign, such as incumbency or name recognition, policy issues, the liabilities of their opponents, and the general campaign environment specific to a particular year.[1] The strategies accommodate long-term factors, such as public expectations about the nature of the office and the nature of the electoral system, and short-term factors, including financial resources, their opponents' efforts, and the shifting concerns of the voters.

In general, a candidate's strategy toward the singular goal of election can follow one of three paths: party oriented, issue oriented, or image oriented. The first is a campaign based on planting in the voters' minds an association between the candidate and a political party. It also includes usage of the existing party machinery to win election.

The next strategy is where the candidate forms an electoral coalition by taking stances in line with various groups of voters. A good example of this strategy in a presidential race comes from 1984. Of all the advertisements broadcast by Ronald Reagan and Walter Mondale that year, 68 percent focused on domestic issues, especially the economy and taxes, and another 17 percent on international affairs. Just 8 percent of campaign ads were directed at personal qualities.[2]

The last major campaign path, the image oriented, involves a strategy where the candidate personally becomes the selling point. This strategy focuses on leadership capabilities, experience, or integrity.[3] The best example in modern times of this strategy, at least as far as television advertising is concerned, is the 1960 race. In that year, 69 percent of the Nixon and Kennedy ads focused on personal qualities, especially leadership, experience, competence, and independence. By contrast, just 6 percent dealt with international affairs and 24 percent with domestic issues.

All three paths—party, issue, image—are intertwined to varying degrees in most campaigns. But the thematic presentation of the campaign may hinge on a single strategy. For instance, in one-party–dominated districts or states, a party-based strategy in a general election campaign usually leads to victory. On the other hand, strong incumbents, whether running for federal, state, or local offices, particularly in two-party competitive states, often do better downplaying party and relying on an image strategy, because voters can be prompted to respond to name recognition or to continue their past incumbent-oriented voting habits.[4] At the presidential level, where the visibility of both candidates is usually very high because of intensive media coverage, incumbent strategies can take on different tactics, invoking appeals to the status quo in good times or personal experience and leadership qualities in times of trouble.

Since the passage of the Twenty-second Amendment in 1951, which limits presidents to two terms in office, most presidential campaigns have involved an incumbent. Up until the 2000 election, only 4 of the preceding 12 presidential campaigns did not include a sitting president seeking reelection. The 2000 presidential election was just such a campaign. In fact, the quasi incumbent, Al Gore, faced the usual dilemma of attempting to claim the advantages of experience in the current administration while keeping sufficient distance from its considerable personal liabilities.[5] This was quite a different task from that of George H. W. Bush in 1988, who could appeal to voters as Ronald Reagan's vice president seeking to continue many of Reagan's successful policies but with a "kinder, gentler" approach.

Campaigning is a process of communication. To note that campaigning is a communication process seems mundane, but this fact is sometimes lost on observers, including scholars, who often think of campaigns strictly in terms of public opinion figures, models of voter behavior, the strength of political parties and people's ideological attachments, and so on. Campaigns involve all of these things, to be sure, but the fabric holding all of this together is communication. For this reason, to understand who is elected and why, one must think about elections in terms of how candidates communicate and what effect that communication has and does not have on the public.

Candidate campaigns marshal their resources behind various modes of communication: news stories, paid political advertising, direct mail efforts, telephone banks, and personal contact with voters through retail campaigning. In general, this communication is either mediated by other organizations, especially the news media, or it is direct in the sense that campaigns are able to deliver messages to citizens unfiltered and unedited by anyone outside the campaign. Of course, most direct communication, such as campaign advertisements, relies on some form of technological medium, but because candidates create and control these messages themselves to a large degree, it is best to think about campaign ads, direct mail, and telephone banks as communication that is unmediated in an organizational sense.

The Internet has, of course, created a new set of technological means for communicating. Actually, some Internet-based campaign communication is mediated and some is not. Online news is an example of a mediated form of Web-based communication, since it simply transfers the functions of news corporations in selecting information about candidates, packaging it, and distributing it to select audiences. It is worth noting, though it will not be our focus here, that the Internet vastly multiplies the number and diversity of potential sources of mediated campaign communication. Virtually any individual or organization operating as a "third person" can offer its version of communication about the progress of a campaign and its hopes for the outcome, though the audience for such a version may be minuscule.

In our analysis of candidates' use of the Internet in 2000, our concern was the function of the Internet as a new form of direct communication, which permits candidates to communicate messages to citizens without the intervention, editorship, or control of other organizations, businesses, or individuals. We wanted to see how candidates had absorbed the lessons of earlier campaigns: that the Web and e-mail allow the candidate to avoid a journalistic filter with its increasing emphasis on horse races and candidate strategies rather than issues;[6] that they allow message dissemination at a much lower cost than paid media; that they offer an audience apparently more serious about its political information than the passive primetime television audience; and that communication can be dynamic, responsive to unfolding campaign events on a daily and even hourly basis.[7]

To organize our analysis of the content of the 2000 campaigns' use of the Internet, we considered the dynamics of Web sites in terms of two very broad dimensions, each with its own set of categories and internal logic. The first of these was the specific audiences that the campaigns attempted to reach. Where this dimension was concerned, we focused specifically on who the campaigns were addressing. As we will see shortly, this involved comparing supporters, undecided voters, and journalists as audiences for Web sites. We interpreted content and functions—the "what" of Web sites—specifically in terms of whom the candidates were addressing and what they wanted those audiences to do, a perspective typical of political science.

Our second dimension of analysis considered some of the same functions and content from a different perspective, that of the candidates' presentation of self. This perspective comes from sociology but interprets communication from a more psychological perspective. It examines the "what" of Web sites in terms of a theory of psychological influence. These two perspectives, audience structure and presentation of self, led us to ask different questions about the campaigns and in many cases to view the same element of a Web site in different lights.

Audiences in the 2000 Campaigns

At first glance, candidate Web site features may appear generic in their audience appeal, particularly since the sites are open to all—supporters, opponents, and those still undecided. This appearance belies the fact that candidate campaigns target certain audiences. In our interviews with campaign officials, we were particularly interested in assessing what candidates and campaign staff believed about their Web audiences. We then wanted to see how their assumptions about the behavior of the Web audiences affected their strategies with their sites. This would then be dovetailed with our survey research in which we would actually speak with members of those same Web audiences. One of the practical lessons of 1998 in the business of political marketing had been the conclusion that Web sites do not seem to provide a way to convert voters from one candidate to another. Campaign organizations had no way to be sure of precisely the dimensions of this phenomenon, but from feedback and comments through the sites it seemed to most strategists that the Web was foremost a means for preaching to the converted and next a way to reach out to the undecided. In our interviews with campaign officials in the presidential race and the state races in Missouri, we consistently found that campaigns designed their Web sites in order to appeal to two basic audiences: supporters and undecided voters, with greatest emphasis on the former. The campaigns primarily hoped to motivate supporters to take some kind of concrete action, such as donating money or participating as a volunteer, and, secondarily, to convert undecideds into supporters. It became clear that the primary motive for the Web site was not to convert voters. What interested us most was how candidates attempted to balance the tasks that they saw as most compelling: strengthening the commitment of their supporters and persuading leaning voters to join their ranks. Consider first the story of how candidates approached their supporters through the Web.

Approaches to Supporters

In our conversations with campaign staff, time and again we observed a simple, implicit assumption at work. Coverage of the candidate's campaign by the mass media, along with other forms of traditional campaign communication, serves to direct a select group of interested citizens to the campaign Web site. Effective electronic campaigning involves doing something useful with this highly filtered audience. As a result, the main strategic decisions about Web sites involve finding ways to engage supporters. These decisions tend to involve two dimensions: providing a variety of means for citizens to become engaged, such as volunteering, donating, or subscribing to e-mail lists, and providing a variety of issues and topics tailored to appeal to specific audiences. In a nutshell, the strategies of candidates can be described as taking the stream of interested supporters arriving at the Web site and providing the right menu of issues and ways of becoming involved to engage as many of them as possible. We found that the campaigns' efforts toward this end fell into four main categories: opinion reinforcement, activism, donating, and voter registration and mobilization.

Opinion Reinforcement

Campaigns obviously pay a good deal of attention to creating and maintaining positive impressions of the candidate. Web sites and e-mail provide candidates a very useful way to tailor reinforcing messages and update them frequently in response to the unfolding dynamics of the race. As new issues arise, as opponents run advertisements that may be negative in tone or otherwise damaging, and as the press runs stories about the race, campaigns seek ways to maintain the momentum they have among supporters.

In some cases, reinforcement therefore means attempting to regain control of a message or to spin events. For instance, the Bush campaign aimed at this kind of reinforcement through a home page feature called "Setting the Record Straight," which included continually updated responses to criticisms of Bush's policy proposals and attacks on Gore's statements. In other cases, reinforcement entails maintaining a sense of excitement through the long campaign process. Regular news updates serve this reinforcing function. Most of the campaigns included sections for news, where site visitors could catch up on the latest activities of the candidates. The Buchanan site featured an "On the Trail" section where site visitors could be kept "informed of the latest news, anecdotes, and photos direct from the campaign trail!"

Another twist on reinforcement involves feeding the appetites of political junkies, who seek regular, sometimes daily, input from the campaign. The main page of the site is the most important page for that purpose because users want to know immediately whether there is something new to see at the site. The e-mail update is another vehicle for this goal.

There is an irony built into reinforcement strategies through the Internet. The new technology provides a vastly improved means for candidates to undertake rapid, flexible reinforcing functions. At the same time, it can increase the need for reinforcement, because it contributes to the occurrence of fast-moving, unpredictable news cycles. At its worst, the Internet serves as a giant rumor mill. News is transmitted swiftly, whether it is accurate or not, via e-mail lists, chat rooms, and usenet discussion groups. Internet rumor movement, sometimes called a *cybercascade*, is facilitated by rapid delivery, interconnected networks, and the absence of standards of reporting information.[8] Candidates easily can become victims of these cybercascades. Bush Webmaster Cliff Angelo says:

People will try to acquire those [e-mail] lists and then flood them with propaganda . . . and try to sway the vote. It can be very effective and our attempt on that was to realize it and see it as soon as possible and then answer it as soon as possible. And the quickest way to do that, and the most effective way that we saw to do that, was over the Internet.[9]

In 2000, the presidential campaigns recruited volunteers to track news group discussions, chat rooms, and e-mail lists in order to blunt potentially negative information. "If we see an e-mail floating around cyberspace downing the Governor," according to Angelo, "we write a rebuttal to that and say actually this isn't true."[10] Rebuttals of information circulated about the candidate can appear in an e-mail update—e-mail lists are seen by campaigns as a prime vehicle in reinforcing the opinions of supporters—or on the Web site itself.

Both major presidential campaigns amassed e-mail lists numbering in the hundreds of thousands. The aim was to disseminate rebuttals far beyond the names and e-mail addresses on the campaigns' own lists. Information that the campaign wanted circulated was disseminated by supporters via their own messages to e-mail lists to which they subscribed or to various political discussion groups or chat rooms online. Not surprisingly, campaigns regularly encouraged such dissemination to people not on their lists. With the ease of forwarding, cutting, and pasting and the assistance of subscribers to campaign e-mails, those e-mails often did appear to reach a circulation far beyond the original list. This means that reinforcing functions can extend well beyond the direct audiences of Web sites.

E-mail lists are a highly valued, carefully cultivated resource. To the campaigns, voters who left their e-mail addresses at the Web site constituted the cream of the crop: supporters of the candidate who had not only taken the time to visit the Web site but also were willing to leave contact information. Even well after the election was over, Senator John McCain told us in an interview that he was still maintaining his e-mail list of supporters around the country because he hoped it might be useful to him in the future.[11] Most candidates started the general campaign with existing lists from the primaries, and they immediately attempted to enhance them. The Bush campaign reported that its e-mail list grew from 120,000 early in the primary season to more than 400,000 subscribers during the general election.[12] The Gore team claimed about the same number of e-mail subscribers by the end of the campaign.[13]

Strategies for building lists varied from simple forms at which citizens could leave information to very aggressive techniques. For example, the Bush campaign encouraged supporters to download the "Bush-Cheney Outlook Today," which would integrate the user's Outlook program with the campaign's e-mail updates. Potential users were told: "Every time you log into your Outlook, you'll be greeted with the latest news from www.georgebush.com."

Both major-party campaigns urged visitors to establish their own personal versions of the candidate's Web site. The Gore campaign urged visitors to "Build Your Own Campaign" while the Bush campaign titled the innovation "My George W." These functions created personal Web pages for users based on issue interest or voter group information provided by the individual. From that page, site visitors could receive campaign information regarding issues of interest, which they selected from a lengthy list of topics, including Social Security, education, and faith-based initiatives. The result was that supporters who selected this option received highly targeted information directed at just those issues they reported feeling strongest about.

This development allowed campaigns to tailor their messages to the individual voter. Similarly, candidates had previously narrowly focused regional and local advertising in order to tap into varying interests across parts of the country. But Web sites offered customization at the level of the individual voter.

Surprisingly, many citizens were willing to provide information to the campaigns. Leaving their e-mail addresses exposes citizens to unsolicited e-mail, and offering names and policy interests might strike many people as opening the door to a serious invasion of privacy. Yet they did these things in large numbers, according to the campaigns and voter surveys, especially as the election season progressed.

Reluctance to divulge personal information may actually be declining as a result of the increased number of commercial transactions in which a consumer is required to leave personal information (name, address, credit card number) in order to receive a product. The Gore campaign found that during the primaries the vast majority of those who filled out online forms to become e-mail subscribers failed to provide identifying information to the campaign, such as address and phone number. By the general election, those willing to offer such information had risen to 50 percent of those who joined the e-mail list.[14] This could be a function of a different group of voters engaging later, but it also could be the result of increasing comfort by Internet users overall with disclosure.

But campaigns learned quickly that e-mail updates can harm the candidates as much as help them and can damage their ability to reinforce supporters' opinions. Too-frequent mailings angered some recipients. "If you start to flood them with e-mails," explained Cliff Angelo, Bush campaign Webmaster, "then pretty soon they unsubscribe and they don't want to hear from you ever again because you abused that privilege."[15]

This problem was one the campaigns in 2000 began to discover how to solve. In the traditional world of direct mail, campaigns simply guess what constitutes the right amount of mail to deliver to maximize responses without annoying citizens, and they assume that every citizen is pretty much the same. In the new process of electronic campaigning, the solution is simply to ask citizens how often they are willing to receive e-mail.

The most sophisticated campaigns organize their e-mail dissemination by voters' desired frequency of contact with the campaign. For example, in 2000, one Missouri gubernatorial candidate had three e-mail lists available—one for frequent updates, another for weekly e-mail announcements, and a third for even less frequent contact with the campaign. This practice represents another element of tailoring campaign communication to the interest level of the individual voter. Not only did these campaigns learn individually what issues voters cared about most, they learned how often they wanted to hear about those issues.

The campaigns needed a rationale for reinforcing messages, such as some bit of news about the campaign. Events often provided that tie. New favorable poll numbers, a major speech by the candidate, and even embarrassing news for the opposition—all became legitimate reasons for initiating an e-mailing. For example, when Dick Cheney was selected by George W. Bush as the Republican vice-presidential candidate, the Gore campaign sent an e-mail to supporters recounting Cheney's strongly conservative votes as a member of Congress.

Not only do campaigns use online communication to reinforce candidate support, but they also use it to gauge how successful they are at reaching supporters. For example, the Bush campaign encouraged e-mail recipients to reply to the staff, which, according to the campaign, resulted in approximately 10,000 messages daily from recipients of Bush's mass e-mails. On election day, the Gore campaign sent messages requesting that people report back to the campaign via e-mail when they had voted.

One of the most innovative techniques to emerge in the 2000 campaigns involved efforts to help citizens supportive of a candidate to find and interact with one another on their own terms. Only one presidential campaign used this new forum. The Gore operation used an instant messaging system to allow supporters of the vice president to find one another and to interact through an online live chat group. The campaign felt that a key way to reinforce supporters' commitment to Gore, as well as to accomplish other tasks, was to put those supporters in touch with one another.

The purpose of the instant messaging system, according to Webmaster Ben Green, was to link supporters by "giving them a means by which they could communicate with each other, identify each other, and organize together completely independent of the campaign's formal apparatus." Their system was most active following key events, such as candidate debates or major news stories about the campaign. Green calls this technique the "single biggest technological development of the 2000 campaign."[16]

Although it was indeed novel, the question remains open whether the instant messaging system connecting Gore supporters had much impact on the campaign's goals. It also remains to be seen whether this approach to reinforcement will be adopted by other campaigns in future years, as it runs up against a central tenet of traditional campaigning, which is for candidates to control "the message." Interaction among potential voters may offer certain groups with separate agendas an opportunity to make their own case to Gore supporters, which might turn out to be beneficial or might not.

Activism

The second major category of Internet-based campaigning is activism. Here the goal of campaigning is to move interested but passive spectators of the campaign into activists. "Obviously one of the purposes of the Internet and of e-mail, frankly," according to one Senate candidate campaign staffer, "is to mobilize the people that are supportive of us and to get them excited about the campaign and to give them a sense of momentum and activity within the campaign."[17] Voting is the final act expected of campaign spectators. But the campaign hopes a small percentage of those spectators will go beyond that elementary act and work on behalf of the campaign, by completing a volunteer form or using the online donation option.

However, just as in the world of traditional media, spectating, not involvement, is the baseline activity online. According to campaign staff, the vast majority of visitors to Web sites do nothing more than click on a few pages and leave. Candidate sites are therefore designed to elicit a response from potential activists. They want these site visitors to do something for them. Web site home pages scream with calls for immediate action: "What You Can Do Today" (Nader); "Your Participation Is Critical to Our Campaign. Choose a Way to Take Action" (Gore); "Help Pat, Help America. Click Here" (Buchanan). According to Ben Green, Gore campaign Webmaster, taking such action mattered greatly to the campaign:

> [T]hat's your measure of success: How many times is a form submitted on the site? What is the degree to which people are interacting with you and you have sort of a two-way dialogue going back and forth between [the] campaign and people who are visiting the site? That's your real measure of success.[18]

According to Green, the Gore Web site averaged upward of 20 percent of unique visitors filling out some kind of form or leaving a message on the Web site's bulletin board.[19]

As we saw in chapter 2, initially campaigns used Web sites to identify volunteers for traditional campaign activities, such as dropping leaflets or hosting fundraisers. Offline activism recruitment was fed from online volunteer identification. In 2000, for example, all of the candidate sites also had online volunteer forms inviting site visitors to volunteer for offline activities. These included handing out leaflets, putting up yard signs, and hosting candidate parties.

Campaigns employ their e-mail lists as mechanisms for finding volunteers. Most of those who subscribe to e-mail lists are not traditional campaign volunteers. The e-mail list thus becomes a tool for increasing the number of volunteers for the campaign. In 2000, e-mail updates were continually sent to subscribers urging them to volunteer in the campaign, if they had not already done so.[20] Some campaigns advertise upcoming rallies or other campaign events.

For example, in 2000, the main page of the Buchanan site featured a list of forthcoming candidate appearances to encourage participation by supporters. The Nader campaign also was active in utilizing its Web site to encourage campaign event participation. On October 17, the Nader campaign listed six rallies and four fundraisers upcoming on the candidate's schedule and urged supporters to attend. Both of the Missouri gubernatorial candidates included a calendar of upcoming campaign events. Reflecting the contrast with the high-profile races, the Gaw campaign for Missouri secretary of state went one step further and invited site visitors to let the campaign know about events in which the candidate could participate.

Other campaigns were wary of even placing a calendar of upcoming events for fear of alerting the opposition. As one candidate's staffer noted, "You have to remember that while it can mobilize supporters, it also mobilizes nonsupporters."[21]

Although opponents can always encourage their own supporters to register for the candidate's e-mail list and infiltrate the list, e-mail offers a less public format for informing supporters and mobilizing them without alerting the opposition. By 2000, such usage was common in campaigns. For example, on November 4, the Gore campaign sent an e-mail invitation for a "victory rally" to its Missouri e-mail list (see box 3.1).

Despite the efficiency of e-mail in reaching potential rally participants, campaigns know they can hardly depend exclusively on e-mail to reach their supporters for campaign events. "We won't just rely on e-mail to let people know about this," acknowledged one staffer.[22] Since many potential supporters are not online or will not subscribe to e-mail lists, campaigns still use other traditional mechanisms, such as telephone calls.

But campaigns have learned to mingle traditional and online activism, as well as group and individual activism. Campaigns want their literature distributed as widely as possible. However, many supporters do not volunteer for organized leaflet drops. One solution to this dilemma in 2000 was to provide online signs and literature to allow site visitors to print signs and flyers to distribute themselves. This development helped campaigns disseminate literature while reducing additional printing costs. The campaign of Natural Law party candidate John Hagelin provided a two-page online downloadable version of Hagelin's 20-point action plan, "America Revitalized." Going one better, the Bush campaign offered a weekly literature piece on Bush, encouraging site visitors to print copies and "drop them off at your neighbor's house, your friend's dorm room, or any place they will make a difference!"

The campaigns also encouraged another form of offline activity: contact with news media. Some campaign Web sites called on volunteers to write letters to the editor or call in to radio talk shows. The Bush campaign provided the addresses of national newspapers as well as local newspapers arranged by state. The home page of Pat Buchanan's site listed talk radio shows on which the candidate would appear in the near future, such as the Michael Medved show, the Neal Boortz program, and National Public Radio. The site also urged site visitors to call C-Span's *Washington Journal* program regularly, exclaiming: "Get Pat's message out there on NAFTA, GATT, WTO, and the New World Order!!! Tell them what you think! Make a difference! Call now! Make that call for Pat! Let them hear his name everyday!"

But the 2000 campaign also brought an expansion in the opportunities for online volunteering. As we have previously mentioned, campaigns encouraged e-mail subscribers to become involved in monitoring Internet content, such as chat rooms, discussion groups, bulletin boards, and private e-mail lists, about the candidate. The Nader campaign site specifically urged its supporters to go online to discussion groups sponsored by news organizations and political sites in order to "help promote Ralph and Winona [LaDuke, his running mate] in these groups." The ease of forwarding messages to other lists facilitated the campaign's efforts to use online volunteers to circulate broadly the campaign's e-mails.

E-mail updates from the campaigns offer continual reminders of how the subscriber can "get involved" in the campaign even if only online. In 2000, almost all of the Gore e-mails near the end of the campaign asked the recipients to do something—either online or offline or both. Box 3.2 is an example of the Gore campaign's pitch to subscribers to take online action prior to and following the October 17 candidate debate in St. Louis.

The Gore and Nader campaigns included an option for the volunteer to help by e-mailing others. The Nader campaign even helped volunteers form their own e-mail lists. The campaigns urged volunteers to e-mail information from the campaign to their family members, friends, coworkers, or anyone with whom they corresponded. A prominent feature on the Nader site was the invitation to e-mail the

Box 3.2. E-mail call to action by Gore campaign

We are asking all our supporters to take the following actions to help get Al Gore's message out tonight, organize for the final days of the campaign.

If you haven't done so already, create a Gore/Lieberman InstantMessageNet account for yourself at http://www.algore.com/im

Identify 10 undecided voters, and have their email addresses ready so you can contact them after the debate and help spread Al Gore's message.

Log on to the Gore/Lieberman InstantMessageNet at 9:00 P.M. EDT. Once you log in, you will have access to a wide network of other Gore supporters who will be online, discussing the debate and organizing to amplify Al Gore's message on the Internet.

On the front page of algore.com, and within the Gore/Lieberman InstantMessageNet, we will be posting updates on the debate, including the reality behind George W. Bush's rhetoric.

Vote in online polls. Internet polls—no matter how unscientific—can influence viewers' perceptions of the debate. News organizations often mention their online poll results when they analyze the debates. Please visit the following sites:
http://www.cnn.com/ELECTION/2000/ Click on "scorecard."
http://abcnews.go.com/sections/politics/
http://www.cbsnews.cbs.com
http://www.netscape.com

Post messages on Internet bulletin boards about your support for Al Gore and Joe Lieberman. CBS, MSNBC, and Lifetime, for example, have campaign message boards at the following addresses:
http://www.delphi.com/cbscamp2000/messages/?msg=1163%2E1
http://bbs.msnbc.com/bbs/msnbc-d2000/index.asp
http://www.lifetimetv.com/boards/election.html

Visit chat rooms to spread the word about Al Gore and Joe Lieberman. AOL has several Internet chat rooms for the debates. Most news organizations conduct online "chats" with political pundits. Visit a chat room, and talk about why you support Al Gore and Joe Lieberman.

And don't forget to:

Call into your local radio shows to talk about why you support Al Gore.

Write letters to the editor of your local paper. You can also post letters to the editor on most newspaper Web sites.

Thank you for your hard work—and your support of Al Gore and Joe Lieberman.

The Gore-Lieberman Web Team

URL for the site to a friend. The preset message urged the "friend" to "please click on the following link to learn more about Ralph Nader's presidential campaign." The Nader campaign even urged volunteers to e-mail news media organizations, "urging them to fairly include Ralph and Winona in their coverage of the race for President." Generally, the Web site was a critical information medium for supporters who visited the site. According to Tim Haley, campaign manager for the Buchanan/Foster campaign: "[M]ore than anything, we used [the Web site] for keeping the troops informed in the field."[23]

Supporter monitoring of the opposition is encouraged online and through traditional means, as well. Via e-mail, supporters in 2000 were encouraged to monitor the more traditional mechanisms by which the opposition disseminated information. For example, some Bush campaign e-mails included the following request:

> If you receive a phone call attacking George W. Bush or his proposals please record it or make note of the attack and report it by calling 1-800-878-9374.

All of these innovations suggest that the campaigns seek to convert site visitors into one-person miniature campaign organizations: e-mailing others, contacting media organizations, posting or monitoring messages on bulletin boards, or printing and distributing literature to friends. One of the major contributions of the 2000 campaign was the proliferation of online campaign toolkits for activists.[24]

One of the major questions that cannot yet be answered easily is what fraction of the volunteer activity associated with the Internet would have occurred anyway absent the Internet. For instance, according to Jonah Baker, Nader campaign Webmaster, their campaign site recruited a total of 40,000 volunteers.[25] We do not know—and neither did the Nader campaign—how many of those 40,000 people would have found a way to participate in the campaign without the Web. At the very least, it is clear that the Web has become a locus of a substantial amount of interaction between candidates and their volunteers.

Donating

The aphorism "Money is the mother's milk of politics" applies no less to candidates at the beginning of the twenty-first century than it did when California political leader Jesse Unruh uttered it in the 1960s.[26] In 2000, all of the major presidential candidates included fundraising sections on their Web sites, and these fundraising activities constituted the third major category of Internet-based campaign activities. Fundraising online far exceeded the success of the 1996 presidential race, when the Clinton campaign site brought in only an estimated $10,000 through such donations.[27] Yet, the 2000 campaigns did not net the revenue widely expected. One estimate early in the campaign predicted that the presidential candidates would raise as much as $30 million by November.[28] Expectations were heightened particularly in the wake of the widely reported John McCain Internet donation windfall following his New Hampshire primary win.

However, this kind of major shift in the flow of campaign funds through Internet-based channels did not materialize. The two major party presidential campaigns raised millions of dollars rather than the estimated tens of millions. Indeed, the Internet sites for smaller campaigns barely paid for themselves in fundraising. The Buchanan campaign manager related that each e-mail solicitation netted only $3–6,000. "So it was probably just barely enough to pay my salary and for the start-up costs, and then a bit more," he admitted.[29]

Fundraising was an especially important online objective for minor-party candidates. The Webmaster for the Nader site told us that raising money was the *main* goal of the Web site. For Nader, as all the candidates with whom we spoke, the flow of fundraising was tied to events. Campaign activities or announcements of one kind or another boosted the flow of funds, which would then fall back to low levels between events. This phenomenon was more visible online than with traditional flows of money. According to Jonah Baker, Nader campaign Webmaster, donations temporarily spiked "tenfold" when Nader gave the Web address of his site in a major speech, a practice which quickly became routine in his speaking.[30] Gore Webmaster Ben Green said: "When they put Dick Cheney on the [Republican] ticket I think maybe we raised $125,000 or $150,000 in a day but part of that was us sending out an e-mail that was pointing out the more right-wing votes that Cheney had taken."[31]

The goal of fundraising varied across the candidate sites. Due to federal election rules providing public money for general election funds for presidential candidates in return for limits on these campaigns' use of other money, Gore and Bush directed donations to the General Election Legal and Accounting Compliance Fund. This campaign-created fund provided money for the campaigns' legal and accounting expenses. Visitors to the Bush site, for example, were instructed that, by giving to this fund, they were helping "free up funds for important programs such as television buys and get-out-the-vote drives."

But minor-party presidential candidates Nader and Hagelin were not qualified for federal funding because neither of their parties had received the required 5 percent of the popular vote in the prior election, so they used online donations differently. Patrick Buchanan did receive matching funds amounting to $12 million because of the Reform party's performance in the 1996 campaign. But the Buchanan campaign also could raise and spend independent funds. All of the presidential sites posted an explanation of Federal Election Commission requirements, such as limits on the donation amount or the illegality of accepting donations from people who are not American citizens. The Nader campaign encouraged online site visitors to donate beyond the $1,000 limit by giving up to another $1,000 to a primary election committee, which was allowable even though Nader did not run in a primary election.

In the end, Internet fundraising proved no substitute for traditional mechanisms of shaking the money tree, a fact illustrated nicely by the figures for the Talent for Governor Campaign in Missouri. The Talent campaign raised $10,000 through online donations and $8 million through traditional means.[32] Unfortunately, for most candidates, precise and reliable estimates like this of the fraction of all funds raised online are difficult to come by. Federal election rules do not require differentiating the means by which funds were received, so there is no central repository of data describing how funds moved from donors to candidates. More important, it is impossible to sort out how much of funds received online would have reached candidates another way absent the Internet. According to campaign staff in the 2000 presidential and Missouri campaigns, a significant fraction of the already modest volume of online funds was simply donations that would otherwise have reached candidates by mail or phone. In some cases, we were told about telephone volunteers working for candidates who may have entered donations received through traditional telemarketing techniques into their financial systems through the candidates' own Web forms and then reported to the media how successful the online fundraising was.

Our own very rough estimate from speaking with campaign staff is that no more than a few percent of presidential candidates' receipts came through the Internet, and that half or more of those funds probably would have reached the candidate even absent the Internet. We also conclude that the volume of online funding received by a candidate was directly related to the candidate's overall visibility in the media. Highly visible candidates typically not only raised more funds through the Internet in absolute terms but also raised more as a proportion of all funding than less visible candidates.

Although not as disappointing as 1996, online fundraising in 2000 clearly was not the gold mine originally predicted. At best, candidates were able to use the Web as a supplemental vehicle to raise funds, and in many cases the benefits of this supplement accrued disproportionately to the same candidates who traditionally would have prospered most. The Internet reinforces rather than undermines the financial advantages of candidates who receive the most attention from traditional media.

Voter Registration and Mobilization

The bottom line for electoral campaigns is getting more voters to the polls than any other candidate. Of course many voters, including those who are Internet users, need to be reminded to register and to vote. Contributing toward this objective is the fourth major category of Internet-based campaigning among supporters.

In 2000, reminders to vote became regular features of candidate sites. For example, the Bush campaign placed visible reminders on its state Web sites to alert voters to various deadlines, such as the voter registration cutoff and absentee ballot deadlines, and upcoming critical dates, including primary elections and November 7, general election day.

A campaign's online efforts to mobilize potential voters begins with a distinct advantage: Political site users are more likely to vote in the first place. The citizen who comes to the candidate site is more political than the average television ad viewer in the opinion of campaign staff. One campaign Webmaster concluded: "[I]f you have a voter who has taken the time to come to the Web site . . . there is a high likelihood that this person is going to vote. So we make every attempt to provide as much information as we can to help to capture that vote."[33]

The 2000 campaign demonstrated how get-out-the-vote-drives may operate in the future: a combination of traditional and online methods. Traditionally, candidates have relied on phone banks and last-minute mail appeals to stimulate voters. The campaigns did not abandon those methods in 2000. They still relied on party organizations or interest groups and used traditional means for reaching voters. Republicans flooded swing states with computerized telephone messages from such familiar party luminaries as General Norman Schwarzkopf and Barbara Bush, while Democrats and their allied organizations did the same with entertainers, such as actress Sarah Jessica Parker, who was intended to appeal to young women. According to Bush's press secretary, in the final days of the campaign, 62 million phone calls were made to urge support for Bush, while 110 million literature pieces and 1.2 million yard signs were distributed throughout the country.[34]

The Gore campaign did likewise, including heavy reliance on the efforts of organized labor. The unions claimed that on election day they had 100,000 campaign workers distributing literature, making phone calls, and driving voters to the polls.[35] The campaign did supplement these efforts with an online outreach in the waning days of the campaign.

By the end, the campaigns sent e-mails to every subscriber on their e-mail lists, usually on a daily basis. The Bush campaign sent more than 600,000 e-mail messages a day during the last few days of

Box 3.3. GOTV election day e-mail sent by Gore campaign

*** Get Out The Vote Mail—November 7, 2000 ***
get wired in to the Gore-Lieberman campaign @ http://www.algore.com
IT'S ELECTION DAY—GET OUT AND VOTE
BRING 10 FRIENDS TO THE POLLS!

Dear Friends,
Have You Voted Yet? Send us an E-Mail Here at the National Campaign Headquarters and
Let Us Know! Today will be one of the closest elections in American history. Two or three
votes in your neighborhood could make the difference between winning and losing the
White House. There are real differences between Al Gore and George Bush on education,
health care, tax cuts, foreign policy, and experience. Don't waste another minute!

GO VOTE!

To unsubscribe from Gore-Lieberman Mail, please send a blank message to:
mailto:remove-56506701–16778997–5weuvnqc2a6am@cheetahmail.com

Gore/Lieberman, Inc.
601 Mainstream Drive
Nashville, TN 37228
615–340-2000
TTY (for the hearing-impaired) 615-340-3260

http://www.algore.com

Paid for by Gore/Lieberman, Inc.

the campaign.[36] The campaigns' efforts were supplemented by other
groups' efforts to use e-mail to mobilize their supporters. For example,
the Sierra Club sent out 50,000 e-mails on behalf of Al Gore to its
members in swing states during the last few days of the election.[37] The
effort was to both educate and mobilize. Last-minute messages offered
information about polling places and times, and they strongly urged
voters to go to the polls.

The online get-out-the-vote effort continued into election day as
well. E-mail made virtual last-minute contact possible as campaigns
reached out to voters throughout the day, targeted at supporters in
various states and by demographic group.

Box 3.4. Last minute GOTV e-mail message

Election Day, Tuesday, November 7, 2000

Dear Friend:

I want to remind you that today is election day. Our generation has a chance to make a difference—to send a signal that we want new leaders who trust you, not government. You deserve a government for the 21st century—a government that reflects your values— your entrepreneurial spirit, your trust in initiative, and your commitment to leaving behind a better world than you inherited.

Our Republican team would provide that kind of leadership. George W. Bush and all of our great Republican candidates will focus on results, not daily polls.

The other side has been running non-stop negative attacks against our candidates. Don't let their fear tactics succeed. Please take your family and friends to the polls today and vote for George W. Bush and all of our great Republican team.

Thank you very much.

George P. Bush

LAST CHANCE!
The polls will close in a few hours. The Party that best gets its voters to the polls will win. Please forward this email to your friends and encourage them to vote. Thank you!

Box 3.3 reproduces an example of one e-mail effort to arouse voters to go to the polls. This message, which was sent early in the morning on election day, reminds Gore supporters of the stakes and calls for immediate action.

These messages continued throughout election day. Late election day, the Bush campaign even sent a last-minute message from the candidate's nephew to its e-mail subscribers nationwide, urging voter turnout (see box 3.4).

Urgent commands, such as "get out to vote" and "don't waste another minute," were generally employed to emphasize the need for immediate action by the recipient. The Bush campaign seemed more sedate in its appeal, perhaps reflecting a sense of confidence later belied by the actual vote totals.

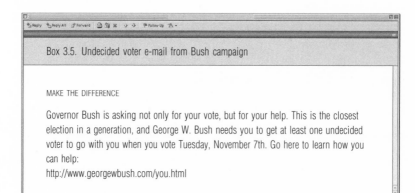

Box 3.5. Undecided voter e-mail from Bush campaign

MAKE THE DIFFERENCE

Governor Bush is asking not only for your vote, but for your help. This is the closest election in a generation, and George W. Bush needs you to get at least one undecided voter to go with you when you vote Tuesday, November 7th. Go here to learn how you can help:
http://www.georgewbush.com/you.html

The use of e-mail was based on the expectation that people check their e-mails throughout the day. Moreover, the cost to the campaign of such last-minute efforts was minuscule compared to the typical get-out-the-vote telephone drives.

But another objective of election day messages was outreach to voters the campaign could not reach directly through its own e-mail list. Campaigns continually urged their e-mail list subscribers to forward e-mails to their friends and neighbors, particularly as election day neared. Campaigns hoped that Internet consultant Phil Noble was correct in estimating that "last-minute campaigning via the Internet is sort of like an iceberg. You only see about 10 percent of what's above the surface. . . . And that's what's happening with e-mail—the cost is zero but the impact is exponential."[38]

Campaigns realized that much of their get-out-the-vote efforts had to occur in this way. For example, the Gore campaign urged e-mail recipients to bring 10 voters to the polls. The Bush campaign recommended taking "your family and friends to the polls today."

Another interesting by-product was the ability of the campaigns to keep close tabs on each other by subscribing to each other's e-mail lists. As a result, each campaign was able to respond to the e-mail activities of the other. The opportunity for immediate response via e-mail was displayed in the two campaigns' message traffic, particularly in the waning days of the campaign. For example, on Friday, November 3, the Bush campaign sent the message reproduced in box 3.5.

The next day, the Gore campaign sent an e-mail update with the subject heading "Call Ten Friends and Remind Them That Tuesday Is Election Day." On Monday evening, November 6, the Bush campaign posted an e-mail message from Laura Bush. The next morning, the Gore campaign posted one from Tipper Gore.

Approaches to Other Audiences

Undecided Voters

Attempting to engage supporters through reinforcement, solicitations for activism, donating, and mobilization on election day dominated candidates' use of the Internet in the 2000 campaigns. The other use of the Internet—persuading undecided voters—took a back seat. The campaign staffs of the candidates whose efforts we examined were typically cool to the idea that the great promise of the Internet in the electoral process is the ability of voters to make choices based on the wealth of information available online. Whereas many reformers and technophiles had argued for years that *surely* voters would rely on the Internet to learn new information about candidates and arrive at better choices, the campaign professionals involved in 2000 races did not feel this to be very likely.

Campaigns just do not see the Internet in this way—or at least they do not see their own Web sites this way. They figure that voters' choices about which candidate to support would for the most part already have been made by the time they arrived at the site. The campaign staff instead hope to influence a different set of decisions: whether to volunteer, whether to donate, whether to vote or stay at home.

That is not to say that undecided voters are ignored or that campaigns feel it entirely impossible that some people might make up their minds as a result of a campaign Web site. Campaigns assume that a minority of site visitors will indeed be voters seeking information to determine their choice. The problem is that the campaigns do not have any way to gauge just how large a fraction of the Web site audience these visitors are. One rule of thumb is that these voters likely become a more significant component of the site audience as election day nears, since a few still-undecided voters may seek last-minute information to settle on a vote choice.

Several standard features of Web sites serve double duty as resources for supporters and as appeals to undecideds, especially the issues sections. For instance, all of the major presidential candidate sites in 2000 featured sections detailing the candidates' issue positions, and in general these were quite extensive. The Bush and Gore sites' issue sections each included about 30 pages of information about the candidate. Visitors to this section could have been supporters seeking reinforcement, but they also could have been undecided voters pursuing last-minute information.

Another feature with a dual purpose is the candidate background or biography, which typically links from the home page. In most campaigns, these links occupy a prominent position on the page. For example, in 2000 the top left corner of the Gore site prominently displayed photos of Gore, Senator Joseph Lieberman, and their spouses and invited site visitors to "get to know us." By clicking, visitors could read a short biography of each individual, learn more about Gore's family and his "road to the White House," or watch a campaign video about Al Gore.

These emphases may be more important to undecided voters, who lack the party cue or the attention to issue positions. We were interested to see in our survey results how the various features of the sites appeal to decided and undecided voters. In the next chapter, we take up that issue.

Journalists

Another category of audience to which the campaigns addressed themselves through the Internet was journalists. Prior to the rise of the Internet, campaigns' communications with the press were primarily on paper—news releases, press advisories, candidate scheduling, and texts of speeches. Now, e-mail updates and Web press information provided these forms of information to journalists. Most campaigns' Web sites featured press or media sections specifically addressed to the press corps covering the candidate. For example, the Bush campaign site advertised a link titled "Reporters and Public Will Get Rapid Response to Gore." The Nader site called its section a "news room" where reporters could join the campaign press e-mail list or search the archives for press releases or news stories about the campaign. Of course, journalists covering campaigns rely on many sources for their stories, including other Web sites.[39] But the candidates' sites offer press releases, speech texts, and the candidates' own slant on the news—all of which together will not be available elsewhere.

The campaign press is not a monolithic group. Two basic categories of journalists cover campaigns. Consequently, the means of online communication are designed to meet the varying needs of these groups. The journalists of greatest concern to the campaign are those who constitute the press entourage following the candidate from campaign stop to campaign stop. During the general election, the number of traveling reporters following a major-party presidential candidate can number in the hundreds. Even for a primary candidate, particularly a well-known one, the regular press corps still can be large. But for these journalists, the campaign would likely shrivel in obscurity. Yet, a candidate Web site is not the best mechanism for communication with this press corps, which was once known as the "boys on the bus."[40]

Journalists regularly traveling with a presidential campaign have little time to scour Web sites for information. Therefore, campaigns must devise other mechanisms for communicating with these reporters, such as e-mail updates. Journalists who are on the campaign's e-mail list receive much of the same information available online, such as texts of speeches and news releases, but it was more effective since it was sent directly to the journalist through e-mail.

This model applies not only to presidential campaigns. In non-presidential campaigns, journalists have more time to consult candidate Web sites, but they also are provided regular e-mail updates from the campaign, although much less frequently than in the presidential campaigns. In 2000, these campaigns typically still maintained offline (usually fax) dissemination of news releases as well, although they preferred e-mail distribution. The more journalists who subscribed to the campaign's e-mail list, the less the campaign needed to rely on more expensive and time-consuming modes, such as faxes or telephone calls.

But the regulars do not represent the totality of press interest in the candidate. Many news outlets cover the campaigns only from a distance or irregularly. Those for whom the campaign is not their primary responsibility and who do not wish to receive regular e-mail constitute the infrequents. For a presidential campaign, this group includes journalists (primarily from local or specialized media outlets) who are not part of the candidate's regular press entourage and only occasionally cover the campaign. Infrequents also are part of Senate or gubernatorial races. They include national reporters and columnists who write intermittent stories about nonnational races, such as competitive statewide races or races involving colorful candidates. In 2000, the New York Senate race was an example.

The Web sites of nonpresidential candidates were viewed as particularly helpful to national journalists who were not following the race as closely and would not be present in the state to read newspaper reports or watch television advertisements. Recent cutbacks in news organizations' commitments to campaign coverage enhances the value of online journalist-oriented information.[41] For the infrequents, the Web site offers significant aids in following the campaign from afar, including news releases, texts of candidate speeches, and even texts of previous news media stories about the candidate.

News releases are common features on candidate Web sites and allow the infrequents to get a current news release without having to subscribe to the campaign's e-mail list. In 2000, on average, the five major presidential candidate sites featured approximately 40 archived press releases each. Hence, infrequents could keep up with the latest campaign news releases without much effort.

Candidate sites also feature texts of previous candidate speeches, both for the public's benefit and for the press. In 2000, the Gore site had 44 such texts while Bush had 46. For journalists, particularly the infrequents, an online speech archive meant not having to contact the campaign to get texts of past speeches for comparison with current speech texts or for direct quotes for stories on candidates' issue stances.

Journalists also can use the candidate's Web site to track how other media organizations cover the campaign. All of the presidential candidates except Gore posted online traditional news media stories about the campaign. Not surprisingly, the posted news stories tend to be favorable toward the candidate.

In turn, the campaigns use the Web to determine how their message is being accepted by the media. This becomes more important for presidential campaigns facing large numbers of media sources to track. According to Jonah Baker, the Webmaster for the Nader campaign in 2000, the Internet was indispensable for conducting research on media reaction to the campaign. "Almost all the research was done through Lexis-Nexis, online. Ralph wanted to know what all the media were saying. . . . We couldn't have done that by looking through all the individual newspapers. [The Internet] makes information pliable."[42]

Campaigns are particularly interested in traditional news media stories that are highly favorable toward the candidate or critical of the opponent. Not surprisingly, the campaign seeks the broadest circulation possible for such traditional news pieces. One means for doing so is e-mail. One press secretary explained how the traditional news coverage was married to online communications in order to promote the candidate with the press corps:

> [T]here was a column in the *Boston Globe* by Tom Oliphant that was about this race and specifically was about our opponent's manipulation of his record and it basically took him to task for misrepresenting his record on education funding. Now that is not a column that the vast majority of Missouri reporters would necessarily look for because they do not have a reason to check out the *Boston Globe* everyday. So, when we see the column we cut and paste it into the text of e-mail and sent it around to all of the reporters that we knew would be interested in seeing it with a header saying "Thought you would be interested in this column." That is something that would not necessarily be sent out blast fax, but it is very convenient to send it out via e-mail.[43]

No matter who the audience members were, it was vital to attract them to the Web site. In 2000, the sites struggled to generate traffic in order to enhance voter exposure to the candidates' messages. The emphasis, however, was not just on a single visit, but on repeated visits. Making the Web site fresh and new stimulated repeat visits because it met the demands of site visitors. An unchanged Web site was like receiving yesterday's newspaper today—and tomorrow and the next day. According to one campaign Webmaster, the front page was designed to "carry the message of the day, the organizing feature of the day."[44] The Gore campaign, for example, wanted to communicate dynamism on the front page and did so by changing text and graphics at least daily and sometimes more often. The objective was to establish a pattern for site visits that promoted frequent contact with the campaign's message. According to Gore Webmaster Ben Green:

> If people went there on Monday, and went back on Friday and saw that the content on the front page was completely different, that would motivate them to check back again the next Monday. By establishing a rhythm like that, you develop a traffic pattern and more consistent usage of the site.[45]

The campaigns also used e-mail updates to draw people back to the site. One Webmaster explained: "We tried to give a headline, then one sentence, and then a link back to the site. . . . You want to get them back onto the Web site, where they're a click away from doing something."[46]

E-mails featured the campaign URL, but also often included mention of new site features with a link to the page in order to lead recipients back to the site. For example, an October 13 e-mail on "Bush News" urged subscribers:

> Read what the former Democratic Chairman of the Texas House Public Health Committee, Hugo Berlanga said Thursday about Gov. Bush's record in Texas: http://www.georgewbush .com/News.asp?FormMode=NR&ID=1723.

A related Gore campaign tool was live Webcasts. During the course of the campaign, the Gore team conducted 65 live Webcasts, which were designed to draw traffic to the site. These events were advertised via e-mail to draw those who had once left their e-mail addresses back to the site again and again.

Candidate Presentation of Self

Thinking about campaign communication through the Internet in terms of audiences, as we have been doing, is very helpful for understanding the basic strategies of candidates and for understanding the rationale for certain functions present at Web sites. It is also important to understand the messages candidates seek to convey about themselves across all audiences.

Understanding these candidate presentations of self becomes particularly critical since American elections have become so highly candidate-centric. In elections that are party oriented, as the U.S. system was during most of the nineteenth century and as, for example, British elections still are, the appeals that parties make for electoral support are based more on tradition, ideology, and the past performance of the party. The personal, affective connection that voters might feel to candidates is more often secondary to these other factors.

The United States has moved away from party dominance in the electoral process since the Progressive Era. The destruction of patronage systems, the replacement of the single-party ballot with a multiparty ballot, the growth of nonpartisan elections at the local level, and especially the development of the primary system have all helped orient American elections toward individuals over parties.

The development of television also powerfully encouraged candidate-centered politics, where the individual person running for office is the centerpiece of a presidential election process rooted in the rhythms of the media. Television encourages voters who are evaluating candidates to place even greater weight on candidates' personal characteristics. In this modern style of campaigning, in addition to interest in a candidate's policy positions and record in office, voters concentrate on individual traits, such as the candidate's spouse and children, family background, and personal likes and dislikes.

This means that how candidates present themselves as individuals to their audiences is a vitally important part of campaigning, in the worlds of both new and old media. As sociologist Erving Goffman has postulated, an individual constantly attempts to affect how others think by expressing himself "in such a way as to give them the kind of impression that will lead them to act voluntarily in accordance with his own plan."[47] Candidates engage in just such behavior when appealing to voters.[48]

Self-presentation becomes particularly critical in a competitive environment where the opposition is attempting to do the same, that is, painting a portrait of the candidate. All candidates are attempting to shape the voters' perceptions of them along with shaping voters' perceptions of the opposition.

There are certain ground rules governing candidate self-presentation. One is that the image the candidate projects must conform to what voters believe is real.[49] A candidate who alleges accomplishments he or she could not have achieved (such as a freshman legislator claiming to have single-handedly passed a major bill or a congressperson claiming independence from the party when she serves in a leadership role) will face skepticism.

Another rule is that the individual who seeks to play a certain role, such as a candidate who wants to become a public official, must fill the expectations of that role.[50] For example, voters expect that public servants are competent to hold a position of public trust, and many voters believe public officials should set moral examples in their family lives as well. Candidates, therefore, often tout their leadership capabilities and their devotion to spouse and children.

According to Richard Fenno, in presenting themselves, candidates must communicate their possession of certain traits: qualification, identification with voters, and empathy.[51] In their self-presentation of these traits, candidates seek to define their strengths—trustworthiness, leadership capability, experience, and so on—in order to convey a sense of qualification for the elective office they seek. They also want to communicate their identification with voters by highlighting the issue stances they share with their constituency (particularly in contrast with those of their opponent) and by emphasizing their common personal background with the voters (such as rural upbringing, parenthood, or being a long-time resident). And candidates want voters to believe they understand the situation of voters with statements such as "I grew up here too" or "I feel your pain."

To make these self-presentations, candidates use whatever assets they have available to them. These may include incumbency, broad

74

name recognition, a favorable public record, or affiliation with the majority party in the constituency. For example, incumbency allows candidates to point to their qualifications for the job. But being the challenger may be an asset if the candidate can demonstrate he is more empathic with voters than the incumbent. Name recognition is an asset in any electoral contest, and a favorable public record can demonstrate empathy with constituents since it reflects constituent preferences. Affiliation with the majority party in the district or state is another reflection of the candidate's identification with the constituency.

In the early nineteenth century, candidates' presentations of self were conducted via the printed word—in essays in newspapers and in correspondence with supporters, who played a critical role in spreading the word about candidates.[52] Thomas Jefferson was viewed as one of the most successful candidates of his day at least partly because of his prolific letter writing.

By the early twentieth century, candidate writing had been replaced by public speaking. Candidates made stump speeches and participated in debates. Still, printed material—favorable news stories as well as widely dispersed brochures and leaflets—continued to play an important role in candidate advertising of self.

Broadcast media, particularly television, added another vehicle for candidate self-presentation via paid political advertising and news stories. Other forms of electronic media, such as videotaped candidate messages, satellite broadcasts, and narrowcasting via cable broadened the array of tools available for self-presentation.[53]

Candidates' embrace of the Internet raises the question of how this new technology affects candidate self-presentation. How has this process of presentation of self been adapted to the online world?

The first step in looking at how self-presentation may have adjusted is an examination of first impressions—what candidates attempt to say in that first encounter with the online user. In other words, how do candidates use their home pages—the user's first glance and impression of the candidate online—to present themselves?

First Impressions: The Home Page

Voters' exposure to candidates is not limited to the politicians' online campaign presence. Nevertheless, given the reduced traditional news media coverage of campaigns (and the dearth of issue coverage even among those dwindling news stories), a voter seeking information about a candidate may be gaining new knowledge of that person when accessing the candidate's Web site. The acquisition of new knowledge begins with the site visitor's exposure to the very first page, the candidate's home page. The first impressions of a candidate's online message come when the candidate's main page appears on the screen. Hence, main pages are important in setting a tone for the site visitor, particularly given the limited amount of time the individual will spend on the site.

The main page is designed to convey both verbal and visual messages about the candidate. For example, in 2000, the overwhelming use of the color green on the Nader site clearly signaled Nader's affiliation with the Green party. Another example was the prominent display of a photograph of Reform party candidate Pat Buchanan with his running mate, Ezola Foster, a middle-aged African-American woman. Buchanan consistently featured a photograph of himself with his running mate on his site's main page. The nonverbal message, important in the context of his anti-immigration policies, was that Buchanan was not a racist.

Focusing briefly on the home pages of the two main presidential candidates during the 2000 general election campaign, we can study contrasts in initial self-presentation. The Bush campaign's first impression online was of simplicity and understatement. The Gore site, on the other hand, was busy with heavy text and an attempt to find something to attract every visitor. While both sites were divided into essentially three columns, they differed significantly on how those columns were used.

The Gore main page packed information into all three areas. The center featured a large, top-of-the-column photo and the lead paragraph of a news story with supplemental news stories (including the texts of lead paragraphs) throughout the column. The left column featured photos of the candidates and their spouses and links to ways to get involved in the campaign or to donate money. On the right, the campaign provided links to multimedia presentations (audio and video of Gore or Lieberman speeches or campaign events) and links aimed at families, children, and ordering campaign merchandise. The Bush center column included information that changed periodically but primarily featured link titles (usually a few words) rather than actual text. The left-hand column offered general links (issues, getting involved, bios, and so on), while the right-hand column was left blank.

Bush's site was considerably less colorful than Gore's. The background on Bush's site was black and white and the menu links were an orange-yellow. The only substantial color on the Bush site came from a medium-sized picture of Bush and Cheney and three or four smaller pictures. The color, menu system, and structure of the Bush main page made it seem more rigid, hierarchical, and structured than the Gore site.

Gore's site used an array of colors, particularly red, white, and blue. Photos of Gore showed him waving to voters, talking to voters, or with his family. The color and busy-ness made the Gore site somewhat more chaotic.

One significant difference was the number of obvious links from the main page. At first, there appeared to be fewer on the Bush site. But when the mouse pointer was placed over one of the main menu links on Bush's site, more menus appeared, giving an additional 35 links leading to sections on how to get involved, Bush and Cheney bios, and multimedia presentations. Bush's menu system resulted in a simpler, less cluttered appearance for the main page.

Gore's home page made those same links more apparent to the visitor. On the Gore site, visitors were told they could "watch and listen" to specific Gore speeches or events. Text explaining a link was more common on the Gore site than on Bush's. One box on the Gore page urged visitors to "Stay Connected, Sign Up for Campaign Updates" while the Bush site link was titled "Get Involved." The Bush site's link to candidate bios only read "Bush-Cheney 2000" without explaining what the link led to, while the Gore site counterpart read "Get to Know Us. Meet the Gores and the Liebermans" and was accompanied by photographs of the two candidates and their wives.

The Gore campaign's strategy seemed to be to make as many resources as possible accessible immediately from the main page. The Gore site placed a small sampling of everything on the main page (audio, video, press releases, photos, and so on). Then, by selecting one of the choices, a site visitor could get a more complete listing of what resources were available. The Gore main page was meant to represent the "best of" what was available on the site.

In contrast to the Gore site, the Bush main page may have assumed visitors would spend more time visiting and would not need to be enticed from the main page. The Bush team apparently predicted that site visitors would invest a significant amount of time on their site clicking on various menus to explore the contents. The Gore site, in contrast, suggested that the Gore team expected people to allocate only a short amount of time and to want to gravitate quickly to their items of interest.

The main page was also used as an opportunity to accentuate the campaign theme. Campaign themes reflect the nature of the campaign environment, including the candidate, important concerns of the electorate, and the nature of the opposition. They have to be credible and more attractive than the opposition's.[54] In 2000, Senator John Ashcroft's reelection theme was "Missouri Values" while his opponent, Governor Mel Carnahan, appropriated the theme "Fighting for Missouri's Working Families." Both candidates' themes reflected the public's perceptions of the candidates: Ashcroft as a strong conservative focused on social and moral issues, and Carnahan's as a Democrat tying himself to the themes of the Gore presidential candidacy.

Campaign themes are featured on campaign literature, emphasized in candidate speeches, and reiterated in press releases and media interviews. Some candidates display the theme constantly and conspicuously on their Web sites. In 2000, two of the presidential candidates did it this way. At the top of every page of the Nader site was the theme "Government of, by, and for the People . . . Not Monied Interests." That theme was credible given Nader's long-standing reputation as a fighter of the establishment. John Hagelin's "Anything's Possible" line greeted visitors and underscored the candidate's minuscule poll standing and electoral chances.

Interestingly, the two major-party candidate sites lacked such a prominent theme tagline on their home pages. By the fall campaign, since they were already well known, the major-party candidates may have found it difficult to define their campaigns in a single theme.

Both sites did, however, attempt to send explicit verbal thematic messages on the home page. Both used a center column to convey new information, particularly to a repeat visitor. The Gore campaign tried to reinforce the campaign's message of the day via the Internet by placing that message in the center of the page every day.[55] But the center column also included other news items on different issues, perhaps diluting the force of the candidate's agenda for the day. However, the Bush main page usually focused on a single issue (teen drug abuse or economic prosperity), which was reinforced at other points on the page.

Finally, one of the major differences between the Bush and Gore main pages was the changes exhibited on these sites over time. Gore's site changed at least daily and sometimes even more frequently. The Gore home page not only featured the date but also the time of the last updating, which sometimes occurred at 2 A.M. Obvious daily changes included the main photo at the top of the page as well as news stories down the center. Only the left-hand side of the page, where visitors could click to become involved or donate, was essentially static.

The Bush site main page updated the date, but the single photo of Bush and Cheney at the top of the page did not vary. These was no regular pattern when information on the site actually changed, but it was certainly not as frequently as the content of the Gore home page.

First impressions conveyed by home pages communicate important messages about the candidates and the campaign. The intention is to make that first impression one that matches the campaign's intended message. For Gore, that might have been an image of an activist who appealed to a broad array of voters and, as the self-proclaimed inventor of the Internet, one who understood how to use the latest technologies available to communicate his message to voters. Bush, on the other hand, offered the image of a personally confident candidate whose supporters preferred the understated look.

But other messages also may have been transmitted. The plethora of available information at first glance might have suggested Gore's policy-wonk nature. But it also could have been interpreted by some as frenetic activity on the part of an underdog. For Bush, on the other hand, there may have been conveyed a message of boredom and overconfidence. Through their home pages, candidates may have been telling voters a great deal about themselves and particularly how the content of their self-presentation contrasted with the one put forth by their opponents, whether these messages were explicit or implicit.

Self: Personal

Candidate presentations of self online can be placed into four categories: personal, issue, support, and treatment of opponent. In an age of mediated campaigns where national and even statewide candidates and voters less often make actual physical contact, an increasing emphasis in campaigns is on overcoming that physical and psychological distance barrier and establishing a personal rapport with voters. We know about candidates through 30-second political advertisements and television news stories. Yet, candidates seek to convey the impression that we can relate to them personally, that we really know them. Campaign speeches are devoted to narratives of the candidate's personal experiences—Al Gore watching his sister dying of cancer, Bob Dole growing up in a small Kansas town, Jesse Jackson being raised in poverty. Television ads also emphasize the personal side of candidates, such as Bill Clinton's "Man from Hope" ad series in the 1992 election.

Candidates now do the same online, using the medium to give voters the impression that they know the candidates. Webmasters seek to overcome the sterile nature of the computer screen through graphics, layout, and overall structure, to offer an attractive portrait of the candidate for the voter.

A standard feature of candidate Web sites is the biography section where interested visitors can acquire more personal background information about the candidate. The biography related information about the candidate's family, educational background, occupation, and even personal hobbies or interests. It is also an opportunity to relate the candidates' accomplishments in previous political offices.

Typically, candidate bios are not written like resumes, that is, a dry recitation of political offices or legislative accomplishments. One exception was Missouri gubernatorial candidate Bob Holden's, who devoted much of his biography to listing the boards and commissions on which he served. Usually, the primary emphasis was on the candidate's human characteristics. For example, Al Gore's online bio began:

> From the simple lessons about work and responsibility he learned from his parents, to his strong, lifelong partnership with his wife, Tipper, to their four children—Al Gore's family is his proudest accomplishment of all. "My faith sustains and renews me," says Gore, "and we all find fulfillment in our families."

The candidate bio is designed to offer an attractive portrait of the candidate as a person. Ralph Nader's bio page portrayed him as a dedicated public crusader. It included Nader's self-definition: "When asked to define himself, he always responds, 'Full-time citizen, the most important office in America for anyone to achieve.' " Bush's biography took the candidate from childhood to adolescence with photos of him as an infant, a Little League player, a National Guard pilot, a father of newborn twins, and a baseball team owner. Most are of Bush smiling broadly at the camera.

Character has, of course, become an overt element of campaigns. In 2000, Gore's choice of Senator Joseph Lieberman was often attributed to Gore's need to bolster his credentials on character. Lieberman's strong religious background, coupled with his status as the first major Democratic officeholder to criticize publicly President Clinton, gave the Gore/Lieberman ticket *gravitas* in emphasizing this issue. Similarly, Bush's avoidance of discussion of his "youthful indiscretions" was an attempt to center attention on his current status as a happily married, religious family man.

Criticism of Al Gore's wooden demeanor had populated news stories of him long before the 2000 campaign. The Gore team worked hard to blunt that image. One tactic for the online self-presentation was to feature photos on the site showing Gore in less formal settings—walking with his family, listening intently to voters while dressed casually, posing with his wife.

Presentation of the personal self also seeks to emphasize the strengths the candidate was perceived as possessing. For George W. Bush, in the 2000 campaign, the candidate's personal congeniality was considered an appealing trait by voters. Surveys indicated that voters preferred Al Gore's positions and his handling of policy, but liked George W. Bush on a personal basis.[56] Ralph Nader's strength was his courage in fighting the establishment. Nader's biography stressed the candidate's record of "standing up to predatory corporations" and that he "fought against insurance companies" and "identified and confronted political and corporate bosses on hundreds of issues."

The possession of leadership ability is an important message to be conveyed by a candidate for president or some other executive office. The texts of candidate bios stress the candidates' capabilities to serve in the office based on past performance, typically in similar offices.

Al Gore's site bio, for example, emphasized Gore's role in the Clinton administration:

> For almost seven years, Al Gore has been a central member of President Clinton's economic team—helping to design the program that has led to our strong economy, casting the tie-breaking Senate vote for the plan in 1993, helping to pass the first balanced budget in 30 years. He has helped to usher in the longest peacetime economic expansion in American history—with over 18 million new jobs, wages rising twice the rate of inflation, the lowest African-American and Hispanic poverty on record, the highest level of private home ownership ever, more investment in our cities, and the lowest unemployment in 29 years.

A leadership trait the Bush team wished to convey online was the candidate as a bipartisan leader. Particular emphasis was placed on Bush's ability to cooperate with Democrats while serving as governor of Texas, as indicated by the second paragraph in the candidate's online biography:

> During three Texas legislative sessions, Governor Bush has worked in a spirit of bipartisan cooperation with statewide lead-

ers and members of the Texas Legislature to enact historic reforms to improve public schools, put welfare recipients to work,
curb frivolous lawsuits and strengthen criminal justice laws.

Now, we will return to the messages that scholar Richard Fenno
identified as critical for a candidate in any electoral campaign: qualification for the office, identification with voters, and empathy for voters' concerns. Do candidates seek to communicate these qualities via
their online presentations?

Qualification

Online messages do stress candidates' qualifications for the offices they
seek. One example—the emphasis on governmental experience—is a
common theme in candidates' self-presentations online. Not surprisingly, in the 2000 presidential campaign, for example, both Bush and
Gore emphasized their respective previous offices. For example, the
first line of Bush's biography described him as the "46th governor of
the state of Texas."

Obviously, the candidate's government experience can only be emphasized where it exists. In 2000, neither Ralph Nader nor John Hagelin could discuss previous governmental office, but the other candidates made extensive use of that background.

Past accomplishments signal the candidate's ability to take action
in office and have become a staple in candidate online bios. For Al
Gore in 2000, his major areas of accomplishment included the rein-
venting government initiative, the environment, and technology. For
George W. Bush, they were education, tax cuts, crime, and welfare
reform. For Ralph Nader, it was fighting General Motors, establishing
public interest groups, and helping enact consumer protection laws.
Missouri senatorial candidate Mel Carnahan's site trumpeted the governor's accomplishments on the main page:

83

> From preserving Social Security for future generations, to pro-
> viding a quality education for the children of Missouri, to giving
> Missourians greater access to quality health care, to making our
> streets and schoolyards safe, Mel Carnahan has committed his
> career to fighting for working families.

Identification

Candidate sites, particularly biography sections, are used to emphasize the candidates' identification with common voters. Here is an example from the biography section of the Web site of Missouri secretary of state candidate Steve Gaw:

> Steve Gaw was born on July 7, 1957, in Moberly, Missouri. He grew up on a family farm, attended elementary school in one of the last one-room school houses in the state, graduated from Moberly High School, and with honors from Truman State University. Gaw received a law degree from the University of Missouri School of Law.

Notice how heavily Gaw's roots in Missouri are publicized. The candidate, the citizen is immediately told, was born in Missouri and graduated from a Missouri high school and two Missouri universities. He also "grew up on a family farm" and attended "one of the last one-room school houses in the state," which established his rural and traditional roots.

Candidate Web sites devoted the most space to issue presentation but still heavily emphasized these personal characteristics. The first candidate Internet site—Clinton/Gore in 1992—contained texts of speeches, press releases, and position papers. But, by 2000, candidates were using the Web to communicate more of their personalities as well. Both the Gore and Bush sites featured online family photo albums—George Bush as a child or Al and Tipper Gore's wedding—designed to convey more typical human qualities to distant presidential candidates.

One recurring facet of self-presentation is the online attention paid to candidates' spouses. For example, all of the Missouri sites mentioned the marital status of the candidates and the names of their spouses. Some candidates went further and provided separate pages for their spouses. Both the Bush and Gore sites offered pages describing the potential first ladies. Attention to the spouse—Tipper Gore, Laura Bush, Hadassah Lieberman, or Lynne Cheney—may have helped humanize the candidate and, in cases of male candidates, may have helped to attract female voters. On the Bush site, for example,

Laura Bush's initiatives as Texas first lady—the Texas Book Festival, early childhood development, and breast cancer awareness—were described and praised.

Another recurring theme is family interactions. Children and grandchildren offer another humanizing element that can be successfully exploited online. Site photos featured the candidates with their wives and children, such as a photo of Al Gore walking down a country road with his wife, children, and grandchild. Some candidates included the names of their children, as well as photographs of them.

The biography section is not the only place where identification with the voter can be communicated. One example is the candidate's image of accessibility to the common person. This image can be conveyed by including an e-mail link directly to the candidate and offering the site visitor the perception that his or her e-mail message will be read directly by the candidate. In 1996, many campaign Web sites urged site visitors to correspond with the campaign by featuring an e-mail link. But the invitation led to frustration as campaigns often allowed e-mail to remain unanswered for long periods of time. Unlike users of regular mail, e-mailers expect quick turnaround. Yet some campaigns either were unaware of the rules of e-mail etiquette or were too preoccupied with other tasks.[57] By 2000, the campaigns had dampened expectations that e-mail would be answered. Only the Gore site included an e-mail link to the candidate.

Another feature is the bulletin board where visitors can pose questions directly to the candidate. In 2000, the Gore campaign site's "Town Hall" section invited site visitors to express their views on a bulletin board or send an e-mail message directly to the candidate. Then, replies were posted on the site and categorized by topic so subsequent visitors to Town Hall could see how Gore had answered previous questions on topics of interest to them.

The replies were crafted to sound like Al Gore. They were written in the first person and mentioned personal references such as "as I have traveled around the country." In addition, a personal signature was affixed to each reply, suggesting Gore actually responded.

The town hall or bulletin board offers the illusion of direct candidate interaction with voters and candidate accessibility to the average voter. This interaction had been anticipated for the Internet; it had been predicted that candidates and voters could interact online, thus bridging the distance between voters and those who wish to represent them. Communications scholar Gary Selnow called the Internet "the one medium that strips away the middleperson and allows the candidates to hear directly from the voters." He urged candidates to "exploit it in any form possible: People telling their stories, filling out polls, town meetings. That's the best spirit of democracy—where candidates listen to the people."[58]

Describing Representative Tom Campbell's online town hall meeting during the 1998 campaign, where Campbell personally answered e-mail, Elaine Ciulla Kamarck predicted that the practice was a "a peep into the future of direct communication—one of the few instances where the full potential of the new medium seems to be on display."[59]

With the proliferation of sophisticated Web sites, including chat rooms and bulletin boards, the 2000 election was a prime opportunity for interactivity to come to an online electoral campaign. But in 2000, real candidate interactions with the voters online were in fact rare.[60] Campaigns concluded that real interactivity was problematic for candidates because it meant they could lose control of the message. Allowing site visitors free rein to post bulletin board messages ran the risk of control by others, perhaps even the opponent's supporters. Most politicians do not like unscripted venues, and the public does not believe that town hall sessions are anything but spectacles.[61]

Interactivity, when it occurred online, was usually scripted. As an example, in the Gore site's town hall in 2000, the Gore team chose which messages to reply to and when they would reply to them. Site visitors never got to see what messages were not answered. Nor did the questioner have the ability to follow up, a function that might inadvertently imply the candidate had not fully answered the original question.

In 2000, candidates did join in chat rooms where there was more interactivity. But even there, limits were placed on spontaneity or possible efforts by chat room participants to divert the agenda. One example in the 2000 primary was the opportunity to chat with John McCain online, but the visitor had to agree in advance to donate $100 to the campaign.[62]

Another vehicle that was used to suggest that the candidate cared about what the voter thought was the online survey. One of the original advantages of the Internet was its capability to create rapid feedback from the public. It could serve as a nearly instantaneous gauge of public opinion. As one analyst suggested, candidates could "learn what interests voters, how they feel about the positions taken, and how the issues affect the voters."[63]

Yet, once again, that capability of the Internet has not worked out as some enthusiasts predicted. Candidates do not rely on the Internet as an indicator of broad public opinion. They are aware of the unrepresentative nature of those who visit Web sites. The campaigns continue to rely on more scientific means, such as surveys and focus groups.[64]

Yet, campaigns want to give the impression that they care about online users' opinions. In 2000, only one presidential candidate site (Hagelin) included an online survey. But three of the Missouri candidates included an opinion poll, with two of them (Talent and Ashcroft) featuring the poll on the main page.

Empathy

Empathy is a message that campaigns seek to convey online, as well as personally. They want voters to feel that the candidate is paying attention and relating to voter concerns. For example, in 2000, John Ashcroft was quoted on his own site as saying he was listening to his constituents:

> During my recent travels throughout Missouri, people have been talking with me about the urgent issues they're confronting. Missourians—from St. Joseph to St. Genevieve, from Greenville to Greenfield—have shared with me their needs for financial and health security in retirement, improved access to health care, and help to fight Missouri's meth [methamphetamine] crisis. With work already underway on these important issues, I'll be pushing hard this fall to make further progress.

But empathy also connotes understanding and appreciation of the individual voter's situation. For example, in the town hall section of his Web site, Al Gore responded to an e-mail using the statement: "like many grandparents, you and I cherish the moments with our grandchildren." The Web site provides another opportunity to express empathy for the voter's position, despite the physical distance between candidate and citizen.

Self: Issue Presentation

Issue presentation is a very prominent feature in candidates' presentation of self online. Campaigns have been defined as "competitions over ideas."[65] How candidates should approach issue presentation has been the topic of a lively debate centering around how specific candidates should be about issue positions, when to shift positions, and under what circumstances it is safe for a candidate to remove the cloak of ambiguity.[66]

But such presentation has become increasingly difficult in recent years as candidates have run mediated campaigns. As noted earlier, candidates have become increasingly frustrated with their inability to communicate issue positions to voters given the news media's interest in the horse race. Even when issues are covered, they tend to be media- or group-driven cleavage issues, such as abortion or gay rights.

The Internet has afforded candidates new opportunities for self-presentation on issues. Because this new medium offers virtually unlimited room for candidates to express issue stances, the limitation is not space but the endurance of the reader. Substantively, this is one of the biggest departures from traditional media messages when we looked at candidate Web sites.

In 2000, the presidential candidate campaigns used this opportunity to discourse on a wide range of issues. All of the candidate sites had Web sections where issues were discussed at length. The number of issues discussed ranged across candidates with Buchanan and Hagelin covering the least (23 and 24, respectively) while Bush, Gore, and Nader addressed the most (31). These sections were accessible from their main pages, usually with a drop-down menu. The very top center of the Gore site main page invited visitors to select from a drop-down menu that covered a variety of issues from agriculture to veterans' concerns. Getting information on the Bush positions was more complicated. The Bush site menu only included "issues," which then led to another page listing a host of Bush issue stances. Each of those then led to a more detailed explanation of the candidate's position.

Since the Missouri candidate sites were smaller and less detailed, the issue treatment was not as elaborate. The senatorial candidates, for example, had 7 (Ashcroft) and 9 (Carnahan) topics in their issues sections, while the gubernatorial candidates included 11 (Talent) and 5 (Holden). They avoided issues such as foreign policy, defense policy, and foreign trade, which were discussed by the presidential candidates. Issue presentation was even more limited for the secretary of state candidates, who addressed only 6 (Gaw) and 5 (Blunt).

One might expect that candidates would address divergent issues based on their constituencies. However, there was a commonality of issue interests—education, the economy, Social Security, health care, the environment, and so on. All of the presidential candidates covered these issues on their respective Web sites. The same was true at the state level. Both the Ashcroft and Carnahan sites featured education, crime, Social Security, and health care on the main page. Both the Blunt and Gaw sites focused on tax reduction, education, and election reform.

But issue discussion was not uniform and did reflect some specific constituencies of the candidates, particularly the minor-party candidates. For example, the Nader site's discussion of nuclear disarmament and statehood for the District of Columbia and Pat Buchanan's treatment of foreign aid and U.S. policy toward China were candidate-specific issue priorities.

The way issues were presented varied among the candidates. While the Bush and Gore sites' issues sections offered descriptive paragraphs of the candidates' positions, the Nader campaign used snippets from speeches or press interviews by Nader or his vice-presidential running mate, LaDuke. Moreover, the Gore site went beyond mere narrative description, offering links to other pages, which outlined Gore's accomplishments on each issue and his agenda if elected president.

But the main page emphasis was most telling because it was the first topic seen by the site visitor. As mentioned earlier, the Bush site chose one main issue to emphasize on its home page. In the snapshots we took of his campaign Web site, Bush's top issue in the center column was his plan for maintaining economic prosperity. The site did feature links to other issues—education, Social Security, and taxes. The Gore site's main page center column (which changed at least daily) emphasized the role of government, faith and values, and the economy with paragraphs initiating the story and then featuring a link to another page where the item continued.

The Nader site treated several key issues the same way. Campaign finance reform, trade, and health care were all accorded brief paragraphs on the main page followed by links urging the visitor to "read more." The Buchanan site home page was filled with discussion of Buchanan's issue stances. The featured issues, in order of appearance on the page, were free trade, U.S. foreign policy in the Middle East, English as the official language of the United States, same-sex civil unions recently allowed in Vermont, and immigration. The Hagelin site listed in brief sentence form the candidate's views on campaign finance, health care, the environment, agriculture, crime, education, taxes, and foreign policy. The Bush campaign seemed to want to focus the agenda, while the other candidates sought to lure visitors into the site by offering a range of topics of potential interest.

Similarly, Missouri candidates all sought to cover various issues on the main page. But the quantity of issues and the type of issue discussion varied. While gubernatorial candidate Jim Talent's main page included a paragraph and then a link to his views on a patients' bill of rights and wellness, opponent Bob Holden's opening statement and the top of the page listed several issues (education, health care, crime prevention, and transportation) in addition to the links used on his opponent's site. While most candidates included a link to an issues section in the main menu and mentioned one or two issues with links to further pages, the Mel Carnahan site offered a list of specific issues (such as prescription drug benefits and cutting taxes), each linked to another page with more detailed information.

Steve Gaw's home page began by discussing the candidate's efforts "from increasing educational performance and ensuring access to affordable health care, to toughening penalties for criminals, improving our seniors' quality of life, and reducing the tax burden on our working families." In contrast, Matt Blunt's page discussed the candidate's personal and professional background but made no mention of issues.

Clearly, there is variation in the way candidates seek to use this medium to present their issue stances. In 2000, this variation may have reflected the extent of issue divergence across candidates or the existence of a few key issues versus one major defining issue of the campaign. The extent of issue presentation may vary depending on the role of the party in the constituency. For example, online campaign sites in one-party–dominant states or districts may include more party than issue appeal.

Self: Support, Affiliations, and Endorsements

Since many politicians are unknown to voters when they launch their campaigns, candidates stress their affiliations with groups or individuals voters are familiar with. These affiliations can be membership in a party or endorsements by particular organized groups, such as labor, business, or veterans. Web sites became another mechanism for communicating the candidates' associations and endorsements.

Party

Party affiliation is a quick guide for voters and is still a strong voting cue, even in the age of candidate-centric campaigns. Yet, online candidate presentations apparently do not always emphasize the party identification of the candidate. In the 2000 presidential campaign, for example, the major-party candidates—Bush and Gore—did not underscore their party affiliations on their Web sites. In fact, they usually did not mention them on their home pages. Most likely, this is because their party affiliations were already well known, particularly to their supporters, who constituted the bulk of their site audiences. But it also may have stemmed from the need to avoid raising partisan sensibilities on the part of opposition-party supporters or leaners, who might have been seriously considering crossing party lines. This is particularly important given the large number of voters who call themselves independent, even though they actually may lean to one party or the other.

Prominent minor-party presidential candidates in 2000 did highlight their party affiliations. Nowhere on the Nader campaign site's home page was mention made of the Green party per se. Yet, the connection between Ralph Nader and the Green party was visually portrayed—the color green was the dominant color on the site. Pat Buchanan prominently advertised his tie to the Reform party at the top of his home page, as did John Hagelin with the Natural Law party.

Missouri statewide candidates similarly avoided emphasis on party identification. Only one of the six sites studied (Talent) included a reference to the candidate's party on the main page. In this case, Missouri is typical of one type of electoral system—a highly competitive one where both major parties routinely win offices at the statewide level. As stated earlier, party appeals may be more prevalent in areas where one-party-dominant constituencies require candidates, particularly those from the dominant party, to identify clearly with the majority party.

The primary mention of party identification on Web sites in the 2000 elections was in the candidate's biography, although some candidates even avoided mentioning party identification there. Half of the Missouri statewide candidates did not mention their party affiliations even in their biography sections.

Groups and Individuals

Group endorsements of candidates are designed to offer cues to voters who belong to those groups. They provide crucial information for the voter about the candidate's orientation and can be influential in conveying the message that the candidate is sympathetic to the group member's interests.[67]

Candidate Web sites become opportunities to telegraph to visitors that the candidate supports the group with which the site visitor identifies. In 2000, the major presidential candidate sites listed various groups the site visitor could identify with. For example, the Nader site particularly targeted younger people, even featuring a section specifically for students, which included organizing tips, news updates from Students for Nader/LaDuke, and student newspaper endorsements. The Nader site also highlighted endorsements of the candidate from specific groups, such as the United Electrical Workers Union and the California Nurses Association. Most of the Missouri candidates also featured endorsements from organizations such as the Missouri Farm Bureau or the Missouri Fraternal Order of Police.

Nonetheless, generally the emphasis on the presidential sites was less on specific organizations, such as particular associations and unions, and more on general groupings of voters. For example, the Gore site invited visitors to the main page to "pick your group." The list included 30 groups, including traditional ones, such as Irish Americans, Jewish voters, educators, and those with environmental concerns. But it also included new, broader groupings, such as the faith community, business leaders, and Americans with disabilities.

Even when groups are mentioned specifically by name, there is reluctance to go beyond that. For example, in 2000 the candidate sites avoided linking to the Web sites of endorsing groups. Such links not only draw site visitors off the site, which campaigns do not want to happen, but they also may link the candidate to group views he or she does share.

The Web site listings of groups in the 2000 campaign showed that traditional groupings have been supplemented by new technology-oriented groups. Gore specifically appealed to the "tech community" by including the group among his voter outreach groups and including technology in his listing of issue priorities. The Bush site, similarly, addressed the issue of technology and the new economy in its issue section, but the site did not separate out the high-tech community as a specific group.

Endorsements from prominent individuals also can be important in facilitating voter acceptance of a candidate. Traditionally, candidates have welcomed and advertised endorsements from well-known entertainers, sports figures, and other politicians. Candidate Web sites become another mechanism for communicating those endorsements from prominent individuals, which sometimes are spotlighted on the site. During the 2000 primaries, for example, the Bill Bradley home page showed a photograph of Michael Jordan and invited site visitors to watch a video of Jordan's endorsement of the candidate. In the 2000 general election campaign, the Nader site included an audio message from filmmaker Michael Moore.

Some candidate sites list politician endorsements, often in specific "endorsement" sections. During the 2000 primaries, the Bush campaign touted its broad support from the Republican party establishment by including a lengthy list of state and federal public officials who endorsed Bush's candidacy. Missouri gubernatorial candidate Bob Holden's endorsement section listed prominent Missouri politicians, such as Governor Mel Carnahan and House Minority Leader Richard Gephardt.

Media

Newspaper endorsements are prized by candidates, given the wide readership and potential effect on voters that newspapers possess.[68] Presidential candidates covet endorsements from the nationally recognized prestige press (for example, the *New York Times*, *Washington Post*, or *Chicago Tribune*), while statewide candidates seek endorsements from major newspapers in their state, such as *Newsday* in New York or the *San Francisco Chronicle*.

To further the effect of endorsements, campaigns trumpet them on their Web sites. These announcements may come in the "news" sections of the sites or they may be prominently featured on the main page. In 2000, both the Bush and Gore sites featured endorsements from news organizations. For emphasis, campaign sites sometimes included the full text of the endorsement or the excerpts that included praise for the candidate. One example of the latter is the *Minneapolis Star Tribune* endorsement of Al Gore, an excerpt of which appeared on the candidate's Web site:

> Under the headline "Al Gore—Prepared to Lead, in the Right Direction," the *Star Tribune* wrote about Gore's "wiser" economic course, foreign policy experience and commitment to protecting the environment. "Al Gore, too, has a keen mind. He is also a serious student of public policy. In his service in Congress—first in the House and then in the Senate—Gore developed far-ranging experience and knowledge in subject areas as diverse as arms control and the implications of genomics re-

search. . . . As U.S. budget surpluses mount, Bush has proposed a massive tax cut, while Gore wants to use surplus money to pay down the national debt. Gore's is the wiser course." (*Star Tribune*, 10/22/00)

In addition to actual endorsements, candidate sites accentuated positive press coverage by news organizations. Not only were these favorable stories sent via e-mail to journalists as described previously, but they also appeared on Web sites, typically under headings such as "news articles" or "press clippings." These articles become a substitute for press endorsements from newspapers that do not endorse or become useful earlier in the campaign before endorsements are made.

Self: Treatment of Opponent

Another anticipated benefit of the Web is the potential for voters to compare candidates. Some neutral campaign sites, such as Democracy-Net, Freedom Channel, and Vote Smart, have been created to offer that side-by-side comparison of candidates. On the other hand, candidate sites have rarely been willing to perform that service. This does not mean opponents are not mentioned on candidates' Web sites. Not surprisingly, in the 2000 election, all of the major presidential candidate sites mentioned other candidates. In a presidential race, where name recognition is a given, a strategy of name avoidance is unworkable. This is particularly true in a competitive race like the 2000 presidential general election campaign. Similarly, the Missouri statewide candidates mentioned their opponents. It is important to note that we chose this state and these candidates for our study precisely because of electoral competitiveness. Mention of the opponent, particularly by the incumbent, likely would be less frequent in other, less competitive settings.

95

In 2000, mention of the opponent by presidential candidates was not equal. The Bush and Gore campaigns used their Web sites to freely mention each other. But, typically, those sites ignored their minor-party opponents. The Nader site strongly criticized both Gore and Bush, but particularly Gore, since their constituencies overlapped. The

Nader home page offered a prominently displayed link to "Gore's Broken Promise of the Day." Similarly, Buchanan's Web site targeted Bush for criticism since some Bush voters might have been potential Buchanan voters.

Mention of the opponent sometimes was highlighted in the online content. For example, two days after one of the presidential candidate debates, the home page of the Gore site was headlined "Fuzzy Math?" The accompanying article's lead paragraph exclaimed:

> In Tuesday's debate, George W. Bush accused Al Gore of using "fuzzy math" when Gore pointed out that Bush spends more of the surplus on tax cuts for the wealthiest one percent of taxpayers than he spends on education, health care, prescription drugs and national defense combined.

Site visitors were then encouraged to take a quiz on whether Bush's tax cut plan was more expensive than the amount he promised for the listed issues.

Similarly, the Bush campaign urged site visitors toward a section titled "debatefacts.com," where Gore's debate statements, called "inventions" on the site, were juxtaposed with "facts" by the Bush campaign. The Carnahan site also prominently discussed the opponent. In his message to site visitors, Governor Carnahan explained who his opponent was and why he was running against him:

> My opponent is Senator John Ashcroft. Senator Ashcroft and I differ on a great many issues. He and I have very different views about whose interests our Senators ought to represent. For instance, Senator Ashcroft has voted against extending Medicare to include prescription drug benefits for senior citizens. And he voted to require senior citizens who retire at age 65 to wait two years before they would be allowed to receive Medicare benefits.

The site featured a section titled "Ashcroft Record Check," which was linked from the site's main menu. In the section, John Ashcroft's votes on key issues were described and criticized with the claim that "you will find our Ashcroft Record Check informative . . . and maybe even surprising."

The Missouri candidates were specific in accusations about the other candidates. The Ashcroft site accused Mel Carnahan of changing state policy in favor of organized labor after the state Democratic party received $110,000 from a labor union and for breaking a promise about how he would raise funds for his campaign. Carnahan, in turn, attacked Ashcroft for his votes on issues, charging, "John Ashcroft has persistently voted against the interests of Missouri's working families."

Both Ashcroft and Carnahan were attempting to define the other on their own terms, and not on the terms of their opponent. When an opponent is already well known (as both Ashcroft and Carnahan were), it is essential to attempt to puncture the opponent's image in the public mind. When an opponent is obscure (such as a poorly financed, largely media-ignored challenger), this strategy is less important.

Rapid Response

As previously discussed, the Web has become a new tool for responding to the opponent's criticisms. First, it enables the campaign to see what the opposition is saying about the candidate. Since the candidate site is accessible to anyone, it is readily available to the opposition as well. Not surprisingly, campaign Webmasters routinely survey each other's sites to see what the opposition is doing. One campaign staffer admitted of the opposition's site: "I check it every morning. Just to see what new assertion or claim they are making. About us, or in general."[69]

Candidate Web sites can be used to respond to the opponent's allegations—whether made online or via traditional campaigning or both. And, via Web and e-mail, such a response can be nearly instantaneous. Rapid response as a campaign tactic has become a standard feature of presidential campaigns since Democratic presidential candidate Michael Dukakis's failure to respond to George H. W. Bush's accusations during the 1988 campaign. These responses have taken the form of statements to the press, which usually appear in the next day's newspaper or on the evening news broadcast, or television advertisements hastily taped and distributed for airing within a few days.

But even that brief time frame has been shortened. Candidate Web sites can issue rebuttals within hours of a candidate debate or a criticism by the opponent. An example of this practice in the 2000 campaign was the Bush site's rapid response to Gore statements in the presidential debates. The following appeared on the Bush Web site under the heading "Reporters and Public Will Get Rapid Response to Gore" shortly after one of the debates:

> Invention: Gore said that Governor Bush is opposed to affirmative action. Fact: Governor Bush supports "affirmative access"—not quotas, not double standards, because those divide and balkanize, but access—a fair shot for every single person. Whether in awarding government contracts or making college admissions decisions, Governor Bush believes we have an affirmative duty to offer equal access. Equal access doesn't guarantee equal results—but it guarantees that every person will get a fair shot based on their potential and based on their merit. For example, Governor Bush signed legislation in Texas requiring the top 10 percent of graduates from Texas high schools be automatically accepted in any public university in Texas.

Negative Campaigning

It is important to note, however, that candidate sites typically avoid discussion of personal actions by their opponents. For example, in the last days of the 2000 general election campaign, a DUI (driving under the influence) charge from the 1970s was raised against George W. Bush. The Gore site did not mention the last-minute story.

Overall, the Internet has not been a forum for negative campaigning by candidates.[70] Negative campaigning was infrequent among candidate Web sites in 1996 and 1998.[71] Candidates instead have relied on content that emphasizes their strengths rather than the negative traits of their opponents. In fact, incumbents in a strong electoral position have no incentive to attract attention to the opponent by even mentioning him. Challengers, on the other hand, more often have powerful incentives to make negative statements about the incumbent. Whatever negative campaigning exists online would be expected more from challengers than incumbents. Yet, many challengers do not possess enough of an online presence to be effective at it.

The Internet does make negative campaigning potentially easier because opposition research has become less costly. Voting records, texts of speeches, past press releases, news articles (particularly regarding incumbents)—all can be more easily retrieved through the Internet. Poor issue stances can be laid bare through the issue section of the opponent's own Web site.

Yet, in the wake of strong media criticism of and public antipathy toward negative campaigning in the 1990s, even challengers must be careful. Voters are tolerant of comparative information but less so of outright verbal attacks on the opponent. Moreover, it is more difficult online for the candidate to distance himself as the source of the negative attacks. While negative television advertising may leave the viewer unclear as to the source of the attack, online negative campaigning from the candidate's Web site is clearly originating with the candidate. Given the steady attention to presidential candidate Web sites by journalists and the opposition, going negative can backfire on candidates.

Negativity may be more common in the future on the Internet. Television campaign advertising also began as a positive medium, and then advertisements became increasingly negative.[72] Perhaps as Internet users become more accustomed to negative tones in Web sites, their usage could grow.

Conclusion: The Nature of Candidate Web Sites

Candidate Web sites began as experiments. In races in the mid-1990s—including as late as 1998—most candidates were unsure what content worked and what did not. The site was often important as much for its mere presence as for its content. Our review of the 2000 races, however, shows that those days are past. Candidate sites now have a niche within the candidate's strategy. Campaigns believe Web sites can make a difference in acquiring electoral support. Most judge that difference to be a small one at best, and they are unsure precisely of the size of the effect of the Web. They believe that the greatest benefits likely come from reinforcing the candidate's existing base of support.

Certainly, campaign staffers believe that undecided voters can visit the site and learn about their candidates' backgrounds and issue positions. But the main messages are directed at a different audience. The presentation of material, particularly on the front page, is designed to signal to supporters (weak or strong) that the decision to vote for the candidate is a wise one and to solicit those supporters for assistance in the form of contributions of money, volunteer time, contacting others, and, finally, turnout on election day. The presentations of self involved in these messages are remarkably similar to the presentations of self in other campaign media. The messages about personal appeal, issue presentation, endorsements, and affiliations are not much different than messages delivered in offline settings.

What is different are the interactive, information-intensive functions that the new technology provides: soliciting online donations, creating e-mail networks, tailoring messages at the individual level, and encouraging online activism. In this, the 2000 Web campaign was a blend of the old and the new. The old was largely a reinforcement of the imperative of the campaign to communicate the candidate's messages and to make a successful presentation of self to voters. The new included ways of identifying supporters and interacting with them. In short, the content of Internet-oriented campaigning is largely the old, while the means for Internet-oriented campaigning are new.

It is important to add a caveat to our conclusions about candidate Web site content. This study has focused primarily on candidates in high-profile and competitive races—president, U.S. Senate, governor. In addition, the nonpresidential races we studied occurred in a swing state with a high level of electoral competitiveness. Site content may reflect other strategies, particularly partisanship in one-party-dominant states or simple name recognition by safe incumbents seeking reelection.

Now that we have examined what the candidates are seeking to accomplish through the presentation of site content, let us turn to whether it makes any difference. In other words, who visits campaign Web sites, why do they do so, and what effect do these visits have on their attitudes and behavior toward candidates?

The Audiences for Election Web Sites

Understanding the dynamics of campaigning online requires getting beyond the set of operating assumptions that had come into widespread use by the late 1990s on the part of campaign professionals and candidates. As we saw in the last chapter, by 2000 campaigns were making quite sophisticated communication efforts based on the observation that supporters of the candidates compose the most important element of Web audiences. But the details of the audiences for political Web sites and how they react to their experiences with candidates' online materials have remained almost a complete mystery both to researchers and political professionals themselves. In politics, like other endeavors, knowing how to target a message based on the specifics of an audience is very important. How many Americans actually saw George Bush's site? What portion of Bush's audience were women compared with Al Gore's audience, and how favorably did men as opposed to women respond to these sites? What motivated people to visit Ralph Nader's site compared with the sites of his major-party competitors? What kind of voters crossed over, so to speak, and voluntarily viewed the Web site of a candidate they did not support?

Size of Audiences

We begin with the basic facts from our randomized surveys of citizens across the United States. About 9 percent of American adults viewed at least one of the seven national Web sites in our study. The Bush site was the most popular at about 5 percent of adults, followed by Gore's at about 4 percent. The Nader site followed at a surprising 2 percent, making it roughly half as popular as Gore's. The Buchanan site polled a distant fourth at a barely measurable 0.5 percent.

If people were not visiting the presidential candidate sites, were they at least viewing several key nonpartisan information sites where they could obtain comparative candidate information? It turns out fewer Americans went to those sites than visited presidential candidate sites. About 2 percent of adults reported having seen the Project Vote Smart site, and well under 1 percent visited DemocracyNet and Freedom Channel. Together the presidential and nonpartisan figures add up to just 9 percent of the total population, because of overlap among audiences. Table 4.1 summarizes these data. These figures can be put in perspective by comparing them with data from the American National Election Studies, which show that in 2000 about 40 percent of Americans paid at least "a little attention" to campaigns through news-

Table 4.1.
Number of people visiting specific
campaign Web sites in 2000

Site Sponsor	Fraction of All U.S. Adults Who Saw the Site
George Bush	5%
Al Gore	4%
Ralph Nader	2%
Pat Buchanan	0.5%
Project Vote Smart	2%
Freedom Channel	0.4%
DemocracyNet	0.5%

Notes: Source is authors' national Web audience survey. N=1,020.
Statistical significance of differences varies.

Table 4.2.
Attention to news about the 2000
campaigns from all sources

	Fraction of Americans
None	3%
Very little	17%
Some	38%
Quite a bit	26%
A great deal	17%

Note: Source is American National Election Studies, 2000. N=1,807.

papers, and 77 percent saw at least one television advertisement. About 80 percent of Americans paid at least "some attention" to the campaigns through all media combined, as table 4.2 shows.

These figures help confirm the casual observation that in 2000 the vast majority of Americans were indeed exposed, at least nominally, to campaign news and information through the mass media. At the same time, a small but appreciable number chose to get campaign information through the Internet.

To put this in comparison with traditional media, it means that the Internet campaign audience is a little more than half the size of the audience getting campaign information from newspapers.[1] And almost a quarter of the newspaper audience visited one of the seven major sites we studied. As a mass medium, the Internet was far more specialized and narrow than traditional media, especially television, in 2000 but was not as far behind print newspapers in audience scale as one might have guessed. The most impressive figures for an individual candidate are those of Ralph Nader, whose Web site drew nearly half as many visitors as the far better funded campaign of Al Gore. The 2000 election cycle was therefore the first when a large number of Americans turned to the Internet for campaign information—not as many as read newspapers, of course, and certainly not as many as were exposed to political communication on television, yet a potentially significant number electorally, particularly in a close election.

Demographics of the Web Site Audience

Who were the voters who went to candidate Web sites? Given what we know about the demographics of Internet users generally, we would expect to find they were socioeconomically well off and were sufficiently interested in politics to go to the effort to view candidates' Web sites. This is to be expected for several reasons: Access to the Internet in 2000 was still stratified by education, income, and age, with users being somewhat better educated, more affluent, and younger than the general public. Political interest and activity is also a function of age and education. The older and better educated one is, the more likely one is involved in politics. Men and women also differ in their use of the Internet, particularly for political purposes. In other studies, men have been shown to be more likely than women to use the Internet for following politics.[2]

The more intriguing expectation about visitors to the campaign sites concerned their political orientations and knowledge. As we saw in chapter 3, the candidate organizations sponsoring Web sites were most concerned with addressing themselves to audiences of supporters and offering enticements to those supporters to become engaged with the campaign in some way. They believed, as a matter of professional practice, that the best approach to a political Web site is to assume that one is preaching to the converted and to use the new medium to try to elevate the commitment of those converts.

Our survey evidence largely confirmed these practical expectations, also revealing details of the audiences that have never before been observed. Consider first the simple demographics of the Web site audiences. The expected level of affluence was readily apparent. The median income of people who saw a presidential site was about $57,000 per year, compared with $43,000 for those who did not see a presidential site. This hardly makes the Web audience rich, but it does position the audience above the average citizen. Political site visitors were also much better educated than those not in the audiences. Nearly half—46 percent—had a four-year college degree. This is a substantial difference from those who did not see a site, about 23 percent of whom had graduated college. That 23 percent that we measured is indistinguishable from the figure for the entire U.S. population from the Census Bureau, as one would expect. More than financial status, level of education was the key socioeconomic characteristic distinguishing the Web audience from the rest of the population. The gender gap is also quite large; as we expected would be the case, men were much more likely than women to be political site viewers. About 62 percent of the election site audiences were men and 38 percent women. Because gender gaps are evident across the realm of online politics, we do not ascribe this effect to anything specifically associated with these Web sites or this particular election. For reasons that are not yet well understood, although general Internet access among women is at parity with men, women are simply less engaged with the Internet as a political resource than are men.[3] The Web audience also exhibited a few racial/ethnic differences, although not as much as one might guess from the popular conception of the digital divide in the United States. About 78 percent of the site audiences were non-Latino white, compared with 72 percent of those in our surveys who did not see a site.

Another finding that may come as a surprise is the age similarity between those who visit the campaign sites and those who did not. In 2000, the average age of the Web audiences was 38, compared with 44 for those who did not see a site. While one would expect Internet users to be younger than the population as a whole, the fact that the average age was 38—only slightly younger than the average age of all adults in the United States—may seem surprising. The explanation is that use of the Internet is indeed higher among younger people and declines with age. On the other hand, engagement with politics and news reading increases with age. When these two opposing age trends are merged, they nearly cancel one another out. The result is that while slightly skewed toward youth, the age profile of political Internet users is more like that of the general population of adults than is generally believed.

Ideologically, the campaign site audiences also differed from the rest of the population. The most important difference was that people visiting a campaign site tended to be much more ideologically committed or extreme. Compared with the population as a whole, the Web audience had a relative paucity of voters who consider themselves moderates. About 27 percent of those who visited political sites identified themselves as moderates, compared with 41 percent of those who

Table 4.3.
Demographics and political orientation of people visiting campaign
Web sites in 2000

	Saw a National Election Site	Did Not See a National Election Site
Female	38%	52%
College degree	46%	23%
Median income	$57,000	$43,000
White / non-Latino/a	78%	72%
Average age	38	44
Party identification		
Republican	47%	41%
Democrat	45%	46%
Independent	8%	13%
Political ideology		
liberal	31%	21%
moderate	27%	41%
conservative	41%	38%

Notes: Source is authors' national Web audience and comparison surveys. N=2,020.
Figures show fractions for each row. All differences between columns are statistically
significant at the 0.01 level.

did not visit a Web site. All of these differences are statistically significant, and they are summarized in table 4.3.[4]

We were interested to see how similar the demographics of the
state-level audiences in Missouri would be. We know that the state of
Missouri differs only slightly in demographic characteristics from the
nation as a whole. The main difference is in race and ethnicity: about
86 percent of the Missouri population is white and non-Latino, compared with just 72 percent of the United States as a whole.[5] Apart from
this and a very slightly higher level of college education in Missouri,
any variance would be the result of the differing natures of presidential
and state-level races themselves. As we found throughout the study,
there were a few important distinctions between the state-level and
national results, but for the most part the nature of the audience was
similar. For instance, among visitors to the Missouri sites of Ashcroft,
Carnahan, Holden, and Talent, 52 percent had a college degree and

88 percent were white and non-Latino. This makes the Missouri audiences even more exclusive educationally and racially. On the other hand, 48 percent were female—far more than in the national audience—and the median age was higher at 42 years. At the state level, some of the gaps between the Web site audience and the rest of the population were exacerbated compared with the national audience, and some were reduced.[6]

Comparisons among the audiences for the specific national candidate sites show interesting trends. On many characteristics, the audiences were quite similar, especially for the Bush and Gore sites. Bush and Gore attracted people of similar levels of education, political knowledge, age, and education to their sites, but the Gore audience had more women and a lower household income on average. The Nader and Buchanan audiences differed from each other and also from the major-party candidates' audiences. The Nader site attracted a better educated audience, while the Buchanan audience was notable for its paucity of women and its higher average income. Table 4.4 summarizes these differences.

Table 4.4.
Individual presidential Web site audiences in 2000

	Bush	Gore	Nader	Buchanan
Female	35%	39%	34%	31%
College degree	48%	47%	53%	46%
Median household income	$61,000	$55,000	$57,000	$66,000
White / Non-Latino/a	84%	72%	81%	78%
Average age	38	39	36	36
Party identification				
Republican	75%	24%	24%	39%
Democrat	19%	69%	59%	49%
Independent	6%	7%	17%	12%
Political ideology				
liberal	17%	43%	51%	25%
moderate	23%	32%	32%	30%
conservative	60%	25%	17%	45%

Notes: Source is authors' national Web audience survey. For Bush, N=529; for Gore, N=419; for Nader, N=168; for Buchanan, N=57. Statistical significance varies.

Political Orientation and Habits of the Audiences

Use of Other Media

One of the most intriguing issues raised by the Internet is the extent to which it supplements traditional media rather than displacing it. It is important to understand whether people who turn to campaign Web sites for information are people who have turned away from other media, or are those who are interested in both new and traditional sources of information. We measured media habits by asking people how closely they followed the campaigns of 2000 in the newspapers, how closely they followed the campaigns on television, and how much attention they paid in general to the campaigns on the Web from any source.

The main finding here is that the people who pay the most attention to the campaigns through traditional media are also those paying the closest attention through the Web. For the large majority of people, the Web supplements rather than replaces. There are two interesting twists on this main trend. First, people who had visited one of the presidential campaign Web sites in our survey were heavier consumers of traditional media than those who had visited a nonpartisan site. About 38 percent of people who had visited a presidential Web site said they followed the campaigns closely or very closely in newspapers, compared with 25 percent of those visiting a nonpartisan site. On television, 42 percent of the presidential site audience followed campaigns closely compared with 25 percent of the audience for nonpartisan sites.[7] This finding lends further support to the claim that partisan, candidate-specific information on the Internet tends to attract the most politically engaged citizens, while neutral information is more likely to attract the less engaged.

The other twist on this general relationship involves differences among those who use different types of traditional media. Newspaper readers were more likely than television viewers to supplement their traditional media sources with Internet political information. In our sample of Web site audience members, about 25 percent of those who followed campaigns closely in newspapers also did so through the Internet, compared with just 10 percent of people who only followed campaigns "somewhat" in newspapers. But supplementing is less common for those who rely on television for campaign information. In 2000, about 17 percent of people who followed campaigns closely on TV also did so on the Internet, and for those who followed the campaigns only "somewhat" on television, the Internet figure fell just a few points, to about 13 percent.

But what impact do various demographic, political, or media use factors have on this relationship? The most interesting group of voters would be those who paid the least attention to campaign information in old media but nonetheless visited one or more campaign Web sites. These are the atypical members of the Web site audience because they are not taking a dual approach (old media/new media) to the acquisition of campaign information.

Using multivariate statistical techniques, we found that people visiting a candidate Web site in our study but paying little attention to campaign information on television tended to have weak identification with a party, higher incomes, and lower interest in campaigns than those who used both television and the Web. Not surprisingly, they also reported that they found the Internet easier to use than television. In contrast, those who visited a candidate Web site but paid little attention to campaign information in newspapers tended to be younger, more likely to be female, and less engaged in other political activities, such as donating money or volunteering. Yet, like low users of television, they too tended to have a weaker interest in campaigns. These voters also tended to report that they trust the Internet more than newspapers and that they find the Internet easier to use than newspapers. Notably absent from the list of factors affecting media use were education and ideological strength.

These data suggest that, for the most part, people in the Web site audience are also among the audiences for television and newspaper coverage of politics, and that the exceptions to this rule are by and large not very interested in politics and have some form of negative attitude toward traditional media. For the most politically interested and committed voters, campaign Web sites simply add to the opportunities provided by traditional media to learn about politics.

The results were very similar among voters in Missouri. In Missouri, 39 percent of people who told us they followed the campaigns closely on television and 36 percent of those following closely in newspapers also followed closely on the Internet. For those following only "somewhat" on television and in newspapers, the segments of the population following closely on the Internet fell to 18 percent and 21 percent, respectively.

This means that the correlation between use of new and old media was higher at the state level than the national level, especially for television. We surmise the following from this fact. State-level races typically receive less media coverage than presidential elections. The lower level of media saturation for these races may mean that a more selective group of politically interested citizens ends up being exposed to political information through mass media, especially at the higher levels of exposure. Since exposure to campaign Web sites is by definition a purposeful act, the correspondence between use of new and old media is higher under these conditions.

Attitudes toward the Candidates and Political Knowledge

If the strategic decisions of campaign staffs in 2000 were correct, then most of the people visiting their sites had already made up their minds before visiting. The quantitative evidence on this question is quite strong, but it again includes a few twists and variations. About 69 percent of visitors reported that they were supporters of Bush when they first visited his Web site, compared with 63 percent for Gore. So it is indeed true that the bulk of the audience for a Web site is committed. But the 31–37 percent minority of these audiences who were not supporters is significant and bears closer examination. This minority included both those undecided and those clearly opposed. The larger of those two groups were the undecideds. For Bush, 21 percent neither supported nor opposed him at the time of their first visit, compared with 19 percent for Gore. Relatively few in the candidate Web site audiences were outright opponents of the candidate whose site they visited, although that number was higher for Gore than for Bush.

The situation is different for minor-party candidates. Far more visitors to these sites were undecideds. About 48 percent of first-time Nader visitors neither opposed nor supported him, and about the same number were supporters. At only about 5 percent, Nader had the smallest number of opponents visit his site. The Buchanan site, by contrast, attracted a large number of opponents, 30 percent. While in the case of the Nader site, curiosity may have been due to voter indecision, curiosity about the Buchanan site may have been an effort merely to follow the campaign rather than to seek a viable alternative.

These figures lead to two main conclusions. A small but potentially significant minority of the audience for candidate Web sites—at least one in five—was undecided at the time of their first visit. So while it is true that most people visit candidate Web sites after having decided for whom they will vote, enough citizens to be potentially electorally significant, particularly in a close race, are undecided at their first visit.

Second, the magnitude of this effect varied substantially between major-party candidates and those of minor parties. A driving factor leading a voter to a minor-party site might have been dissatisfaction with the two major-party presidential candidates and genuine curiosity about other options. The fact that half of first-time visitors to Ralph Nader's Web site had not yet formed a candidate preference made the potential dynamics of his site much different from those of Bush and Gore. This indecision over a minor-party candidate is not unexpected, since the major-party candidates receive vastly greater attention from the mass media. Particularly with the son and namesake of a former president running against the incumbent vice president, the mismatch in baseline voter familiarity between major- and minor-party candidates at the outset of the campaign season was considerable.

In Missouri, the level of viewer commitment to the candidate sponsoring the site was even higher than in the national races. About 81 percent of visitors to the Web site of Mel Carnahan for U.S. Senate had decided to vote for him before they visited. For his opponent, incumbent and later U.S. Attorney General John Ashcroft, the figure was even higher: 85 percent. In the Missouri gubernatorial race, 71 percent of the first-time Holden audience and 85 percent of the Talent audience were supporters. Although our surveys do not provide direct evidence about why the audiences of state candidates would be even more strongly committed, we again surmise that this is the result of mass media effects. In races where mass media coverage of candidates is less intensive, fewer voters have information about the campaigns, and so those likely to find their way to a campaign site are likely to be even more exclusive.

The level of political knowledge of visitors to campaign Web sites has been one of the important mysteries about the politics of the new media. In 2000, clearly, candidate site audiences were more knowledgeable about American democracy than people who did not see a campaign site. On our quiz of political knowledge, the overall score of the national Web site audience was 5.2, compared with 4.1 for people who did not see a site, meaning that, on average, the Web site audience scored about 5 out of 6 questions correctly, compared with 4 out of 6 for those who did not visit a site.[8] The same was true for the Missouri voters. Among the presidential audiences, there were no important differences, although the Bush and Nader audiences were slightly more knowledgeable than the rest.[9]

As one would expect, those with more education scored higher on the political knowledge index, and older citizens scored higher than younger ones. There were also a number of differences in knowledge associated with other characteristics, including gender and income. When one accounts for interrelationships among some of these characteristics—such as the fact that education and income are correlated—people with five characteristics tended to score higher on political knowledge: those with more education, men, older people, those with more interest in the campaigns, and those with more income. Women visiting campaign Web sites tended to be slightly less politically knowledgeable than men, even when differences in education and income between men and women are taken into consideration.

In addition to our factual knowledge test given to survey respondents, we also measured political knowledge in another, more subjective way. We asked the audiences for each of the presidential Web sites to give us a self-assessment of how much they knew about that candidate before they visited his Web site for the first time. This technique does not indicate *what* people knew, and it does not provide a reliable way to compare these visitors with the public at large. It does, however, provide a useful way to compare across the four candidates' audiences.

The results are intriguing. As we expected, large majorities of the Bush and Gore audiences (64 percent and 71 percent, respectively) reported being reasonably knowledgeable about the candidates before their first visit. This is less so for the Nader and Buchanan audiences. Just under half of the Nader audience reported being knowledgeable about him as a candidate, compared with 57 percent for the Buchanan audience. As table 4.5 shows, only about 3 percent of the Bush and Gore audiences said they knew nothing before their first visit, compared with 10 percent of the Nader audience and 15 percent of the Buchanan audience.

At the state level, the general picture is again the same. The audiences for the Ashcroft and Carnahan Senate campaigns reported that they were very familiar with the candidates, as one might expect for a race between an incumbent senator and the incumbent governor. In fact, the audiences for these candidates reported substantially more familiarity with them than the audiences for Bush and Gore at the national level: 45 percent reported that they "knew a great deal about" Ashcroft and another 31 percent that they "knew about" him. Carnahan's audience was similar at 39 percent and 42 percent, respectively. For both, only 5 percent of their audiences—very similar to the Bush and Gore figures—reported that they knew nothing about the candidate when they first visited his site. In Missouri, the audiences for the Holden-Talent governor's race were very comparable to the Nader

Table 4.5.
Self-reported knowledge about the candidate before first visit: presidential race

	Bush Audience	Gore Audience	Nader Audience	Buchanan Audience
Knew a great deal about the candidate	24%	30%	12%	19%
Knew about the candidate	40%	41%	37%	38%
Knew only a little about the candidate	34%	26%	42%	29%
Did not know anything about the candidate	3%	3%	10%	15%

Notes: Source is authors' national Web audience survey. For Bush, N=508; Gore, N=395; Nader, N=161; Buchanan, N=53. Statistical significance varies. Totals do not add exactly to 100% due to rounding.

Table 4.6.
Self-reported knowledge about the candidate before first visit: Missouri Senate and governor races

	Ashcroft Audience	Carnahan Audience	Holden Audience	Talent Audience
Knew a great deal about the candidate	45%	39%	14%	20%
Knew about the candidate	31%	42%	30%	30%
Knew only a little about the candidate	19%	15%	34%	27%
Did not know anything about the candidate	5%	5%	22%	23%

Notes: Source is authors' Missouri survey. For Ashcroft, N=84; Carnahan, N=74; Holden, N=50; Talent, N=94. Statistical significance varies. Totals do not add exactly to 100% due to rounding.

and Buchanan audiences, with about 14 percent of Holden's audience and 20 percent of Talent's saying they knew a great deal about him. Table 4.6 summarizes the figures for the Missouri races.

Taken together, these two approaches to measuring political knowledge paint an interesting picture. In general, people viewing campaign sites are politically well informed. Among candidate sites, the minor-party candidates tend to attract a larger segment of people who know little about the candidate in advance. The evidence is quite clear that at best only a few voters visit Web sites in order to become familiar with a candidate unknown to them; to the extent that this kind of knowledge seeking does occur, it is focused on candidates who receive the least attention from the mass media or are otherwise least familiar to the public.

114   Motivation for Visiting Web Sites

What draws people to Web sites in the first place? What do they want to know, and what do they learn once they view them? Is a site visit a form of entertainment or political recreation? Do voters have still other purposes in mind?

From among possible motivations—such as learning about the candidate as an individual, obtaining news about the campaign, learning about the candidate's positions on issues, obtaining campaign material or paraphernalia, or just browsing—the most common reason was the last. Nearly a third of respondents gave this as their purpose for first visiting a candidate site. Another eighth of respondents gave a related response, saying that they visited the site because they liked the candidate or the party, suggesting that their use of the Web site was somehow recreational for them.

This response conforms to the nature of Internet use by many people. Browsing is a common recreational activity. Site visitors might have been prompted by a news media story, a political advertisement, or even a casual social conversation to look up a candidate site and merely browse. Once again, this undermines the theory that visiting a campaign Web site is the result of a conscious search for candidate information, particularly in order to make a vote choice.

The next most common reaction was a desire to learn about issues. In fact, this response topped "browsing" among visitors to the Gore and Nader sites. Viewers also were more interested in learning about issues than about the candidates as individuals. As table 4.7 shows, many more people reported to us that they visited a site to learn about issues than reported visiting to learn about the candidate as an individual. This undoubtedly reflects the fact that news coverage in cam-

Table 4.7.
Main reason for visiting a candidate's campaign site for the first time

	Bush	Gore	Nader	Buchanan
Just to browse with no specific purpose in mind	31%	26%	23%	25%
Learning about the candidate's issue positions	29%	30%	32%	15%
In order to obtain general information about the campaign	16%	23%	24%	37%
Because I like the candidate or party	8%	12%	12%	11%
Learning about the candidate as an individual	5%	3%	1%	0%
Because of the design of the site or some unique feature of its content	5%	2%	1%	2%
Obtaining news about the candidate	3%	3%	2%	3%
To obtain campaign paraphernalia				
Donating or volunteering	1%	0%	1%	0%

Notes: Source is authors' national Web audience survey. Figures show fraction of visitors to the candidate's Web site offering each purpose as the primary reason they went to the site for the first time. N=1,020. Statistical significance varies.

paigns as well as candidate advertising and campaign rhetoric in traditional media are more highly focused on the candidate as a person than on the candidate's positions on issues. People listed reasons involving obtaining news about the candidate quite infrequently.

The search for knowledge about candidate issue positions points to some voter dissatisfaction with traditional media coverage. As we discussed in chapter 1, the trend toward less and less coverage of policy issues in campaigns appears to have led some voters, particularly those more interested in following campaigns, to search for alternative sources. Many Internet users appear to be turning to candidates' Web sites in order to learn the kind of substantive information they do not receive when traditional news media focus on personal issues and the campaign horse race.

One reason for which campaigns hope voters visit their sites— involvement—appeared less frequently. About 1 percent of respondents said they visited the site because they were interested in donating or volunteering. Since about 1–5 percent of all citizens viewed any one of the presidential sites, a rough estimate would indicate that a national campaign Web site can reach about one one-hundredth to one-twentieth of 1 percent of Americans as potential donors or volunteers. Of course, many people who first visit a Web site with an interest in volunteering or donating do not end up taking any action. Although some do take the opportunity to volunteer even though that was not their primary reason for visiting the site.

Site visitors' motivations were affected by several factors. Simply put, we found that the less strong a site visitor's prior preference for a candidate, the more important were learning about issue positions and learning about the individual in visiting the site. Among people inclined to vote, but not strongly decided, for Bush or Gore, 45 percent listed learning about issue positions and 9 percent listed learning about the individual as their reason for visiting the candidate's site, compared with 26 percent and 3 percent, respectively, for those who already had a strong candidate preference.

Another factor affecting motivations was overall level of interest in the campaigns. We assessed how interested people felt in the campaigns and found that those voters most likely to visit a campaign site in order to learn about issues were not those most interested nor those least interested, but those with a moderate level of interest in the campaigns. We do not have a clear understanding of why this is the case. The most likely possibility revolves around the observation that issue information has different meanings for voters than personal information about candidates. A relatively flat relationship between level of interest and pursuit of candidate-specific information suggests that mass media coverage of candidates saturates citizens, leaving comparatively little curiosity about who candidates are but a potentially moderate level of potential curiosity about issue positions, at least among some people. That level of interest in issues is a function of voters' overall political interest. For those with little interest in politics in general, there is comparatively less motivation to learn about issues. That is, if one does not care about politics, picking up information about issues at a Web site is probably less important than merely browsing for curiosity's sake. At the same time, those with comparatively high interest in politics may already feel sufficiently knowledgeable about issues that learning more is not such an important motivation. This leaves voters with a moderate level of interest just intrigued enough to seek out issue information.

While it would seem intuitive that voters who had not yet decided whom they would vote for might visit Web sites for different reasons than those who had decided, for the most part this is not the case. The results, which are shown in table 4.8, reveal few systematic differences between these groups in motivations for first visiting a Web site. On just a few of the individual items do differences appear. For Bush and Gore, undecided voters were indeed more likely to seek issue information than decided voters, but this was not true for Nader. Voters undecided about Nader were actually more likely than decided voters to be just browsing for no particular reason at the Nader site. As a whole, when all of the categories are considered together, there are no statistically significant differences between decided and undecided audiences for any of the candidates.

Partisanship is important in affecting why people view candidate Web sites. We divided motivations for visiting into two categories: purposive (learning about the candidate's issue positions, obtaining general information about the campaign, learning about the candidate as an individual, obtaining news about the candidate, obtaining cam-

Table 4.8.

Relationship between vote decision and reason for first visiting a candidate's site

	Bush		Gore		Nader	
	Undecided	Decided	Undecided	Decided	Undecided	Decided
Browsing	27%	32%	27%	25%	31%	18%
Issue positions	35%	28%	40%	28%	30%	36%
General information	22%	15%	26%	23%	27%	24%
Like the candidate	3%	8%	1%	13%	10%	14%
Learn about candidate	8%	4%	3%	3%	1%	1%
Site feature or design	3%	5%	0%	2%	0%	3%
Candidate news	3%	4%	1%	3%	1%	3%
Paraphernalia	0%	2%	0%	1%	0%	0%
Donate / Volunteer	0%	1%	0%	0%	0%	1%

Notes: Source is authors' national Web audience survey. Figures show fraction of visitors to the candidate's Web site offering each purpose as the primary reason they went to the site for the first time as a function of whether the visitor was decided about the candidate (for or against) or undecided. Buchanan figures are omitted because the number of visitors to his site in each category was too small to produce meaningful percentages. Sample sizes and statistical significance are as follows: for Bush, N=498, Chi Sq.=16, p=10; for Gore, N=389, Chi Sq.=13, p=16; for Nader, N=154, Chi Sq.=8, p=.42.

paign paraphernalia, and donating or volunteering) and nonpurposive (just browsing, because I like the candidate as an individual, or because of the design of the site or some unique feature). When we compared people as to whether their visit was purposive or not, we found that the stronger the partisan identification, the more likely that the main reason for visiting a site is nonpurposive. This relationship is shown in figure 4.1, and it suggests that more strongly partisan voters visit Web sites mainly for recreational or nonserious reasons, while those with less partisan commitments are more likely to go to Web sites for information or to take action.

This relationship is not necessarily the one that might seem intuitive, but it makes sense in the following way. If the voter lacks a strong partisan preference, the search for election information may be a more serious and essential effort, while the voter who already has a strong cue for voting knows she only needs that cue, which is conveniently provided on the ballot on election day. Hence, seeking election-related information is more a light activity than a serious endeavor to make a vote choice.

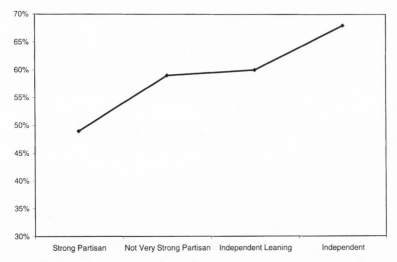

Figure 4.1. Effect of partisanship on the reason for visiting a presidential campaign site for the first time. The line shows the fraction of respondents at each level of partisanship reporting a purposive rather than recreational reason for first visiting a Web site. N=1,020.

Crossing over to View Multiple Sites

The overall portrait of visitors to campaign Web sites so far looks as follows. Web site visitors tend to be fairly strong partisans, knowledgeable about politics, and already committed to a candidate. They visit their favored candidate's Web site to browse, to learn about issues, or perhaps for other reasons. In other words, the vast majority of visitors to Web sites come from the candidate's own base of supporters.

This is not universally true, however. A minority of site visitors are supporters of an opposed candidate. The activities of these people are intriguing precisely because this phenomenon violates the general rule. We refer to this activity as crossover viewing of Web sites. Crossover viewing presents the campaign with an audience possessing different interests from the base, who are likely to respond to different kinds of appeals and information, if at all. Among the combined audiences for the candidates' Web sites, a large minority saw more than one site, and the figures for multiple-site viewing help put the crossover audience in perspective.

Setting aside the tiny audience for the Buchanan site, about 37 percent of the Bush audience, 49 percent of the Gore audience, and 50 percent of the Nader audience saw more than one site. Figure 4.2 depicts the overlap in these national audiences graphically. At the state level, audience overlap was quite a bit smaller. In the Senate race, only 25 percent of the Carnahan audience saw the Ashcroft site, and 20 percent of Ashcroft's audience viewed the Carnahan site. For governor, the figures are 22 percent for the Talent audience and a much larger 40 percent for Holden.

Crossover viewers represent the zones of intersection in figure 4.2. Crossover viewers were younger and were less strong partisans. The average age of crossovers was 36, compared with 39 for same-party viewers. Only 21 percent of crossover viewers considered themselves strongly Democrats or Republicans, compared with 79 percent of same-party viewers.[10]

Who is more likely to be a crossover viewer: a strong partisan or a weak one? In research on traditional media, Diana Mutz and Paul Martin examined how often people were exposed to political arguments or ideas they disagreed with in newspaper articles, on television, and on talk shows. They compared these media with interpersonal networks, the others with whom people talked about politics in the

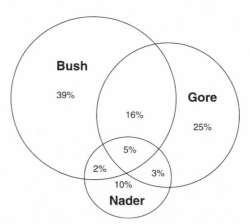

Figure 4.2. Audience overlap at the presidential level. Figures show the percentage of all visitors to the Bush, Gore, and Nader sites in our national sample falling into each of the seven possible combinations of sites.

Table 4.9.
The crossover audience for each candidate's Web site

	Bush	Gore	Nader	Buchanan
Female	41%	29%	34%	33%
College degree	46%	57%	60%	32%
Median income	$55,000	$64,000	$63,000	$66,000
White / non-Latino/a	79%	81%	75%	89%
Average age	34	38	37	35
Political ideology				
liberal	51%	13%	12%	53%
moderate	27%	23%	41%	32%
conservative	22%	64%	47%	14%
Political awareness	5.1	5.7	5.9	5.1
Fraction of total Web audience that were crossovers	19%	24%	23%	49%

Notes: Source is authors' national Web audience survey. Figures show demographics of people viewing each candidate's Web site who report partisan identification other than that of the candidate himself. For Bush, N=102; for Gore, N=99; for Nader, N=38; for Buchanan, N=28. Statistical significance varies.

workplace, in voluntary associations, and in other contexts. The results showed that the more control people had over their exposure to political information, the less likely they were to be exposed to ideas dissimilar to their own, with strong partisans experiencing the greatest selectivity and independents the least.[11] They also found Republicans slightly more likely than Democrats to avoid dissimilar or disconfirming information. This relationship is graphically depicted in figure 4.3, and it is generally consistent with years of research into how people interact with information sources.

Our own data show that this tendency from the world of traditional media has carried over into the world of online political information. Our crossover data allowed us to compare the frequencies with which strong and weak partisans as well as independents visited the Web site of a candidate to whom they felt opposed or who represented a party other than their own. There are three main results from this comparison. Weak Democrats and Republicans were indeed more likely to cross over than strong Democrats and Republicans. All Democrats combined were more likely than Republicans combined to

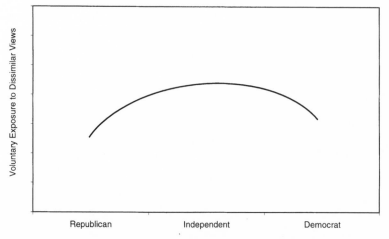

Figure 4.3. Theoretical relationship between partisanship and voluntary exposure to dissimilar political views. Source is Diana C. Mutz and Paul S. Martin, "Facilitating Communication across Lines of Political Difference: The Role of Mass Media," *American Political Science Review* 95, no. 1 (2001): 97–114.

cross over, and independents were more likely to cross over than Republicans or Democrats. The only slight deviation from our theoretical expectations is that independents and weak Republicans crossed over at about the same rate, while weak Democrats were even more likely than independents to cross over. Figure 4.4 shows this relationship from the survey, which provides a reasonably close fit to our expectations from the world of traditional media.

The most intriguing and potentially important question one might ask about these crossover viewers is why they visited these Web sites. Were they considering a vote switch, or just curious about what the other side had to say?

The evidence on this question is quite unequivocal. Crossover viewers tended to have stronger rather than weaker presidential preferences compared with those who did not cross over, but their reasons for visiting the site differed little from those others. For Bush, Gore, and Nader, voters who opposed each candidate were actually more likely than supporters or undecided voters to seek issue information. The fact that these voters also tend to pay more attention to campaigns on the Internet than do party-loyal voters helps round out the picture.

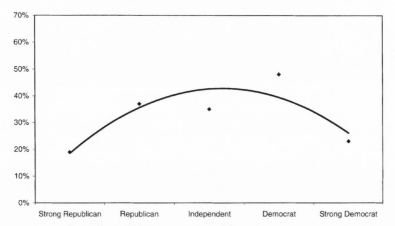

Figure 4.4. Actual relationship between partisanship and crossover viewing of presidential Web sites. Source is authors' national Web audience survey. The vertical axis shows the fraction of each category of partisans who viewed a Web site of a candidate either of another party or to whom they felt opposed. $R^2=0.73$; N=853.

For strong partisans with clear political preferences, browsing the Web is a form of political recreation, and this recreation included taking a look at the Web sites of candidates whom they opposed.

Summary

The campaign strategies of candidates in 2000, as we saw in chapter 3, involved targeting audiences of supporters through the Web, on the assumption that the only significant body of voters likely to visit a campaign Web site would be a candidate's own base. This assumption evolved, as we saw in chapter 2, from the lessons of the elections of 1992–1998 and from the primary experience with the Internet in 2000. The data presented in this chapter provide quite convincing evidence that campaign professionals are generally right in their assumptions about the Internet. For the most part, our surveys showed that the audience of any particular campaign Web site is likely to be overwhelmingly composed of knowledgeable, interested, partisan supporters of the candidate.

This is not the whole story, however. A small but nontrivial audience for any particular site is composed of nonsupporters, and this audience was quite large in at least one case: the Nader campaign. More important, substantial numbers of both supporters of candidates and undecided voters were looking to learn about issues when they went to Web sites—especially the minority made up of undecideds. In an age of increasingly superficial and candidate-centric campaigning facilitated by the last media revolution—television—the solid place that interest in issues occupies in the minds of voters visiting campaign Web sites is an intriguing finding. It is one to which we will return.

Since most of the campaign audience on the Internet consists of people with a clear preference among candidates, the question we posed at the beginning of chapter 3 remains important: Does the Internet gain votes for candidates? Our research about the composition of the audience suggests it does not, but to see whether that is really the case, one needs to inquire into the effects that Web sites have on their audiences.

Consequences of Election Web Sites

Does visiting a campaign Web site influence people? Does a Web site visit affect how much and what voters know about candidates? Does it help shape their feelings toward candidates or their votes?

The picture that emerged in the last chapter shows that audiences for campaign Web sites are composed of well-informed, politically interested citizens, most of whom (but not all) have quite clear preferences among candidates. For that very reason, one should expect that whatever effects Web sites have on their audiences are likely subtle. Rather than persuading large numbers of voters to change their minds, or even helping undecided voters choose a candidate, Web sites are likely to influence citizens on a small scale and in nuanced ways, at best. In this chapter, we turn to these "so what?" issues.

The ultimate goal of candidates' use of Web sites is to strengthen the commitment of voters in some way. How that might happen can be broken down along a hierarchy of potential effects of Web sites, from the least to the most consequential politically. The first of these simply involves motivating a site visitor to return. This is perhaps the least consequential way in which a site could influence its audience, but it is potentially important because it creates the opportunity for the candidate to influence the citizen in some other way. Campaign sites have a large potential for influencing behavior at this nominal level. Beyond merely motivating return visits, Web sites have the potential to affect the audience's knowledge and to influence feelings about the candidates. The sponsors of Web sites—candidate campaigns—place much emphasis on providing content that features information about and arguments in support of their candidates. Indeed, by all accounts, Web sites stand out as different from traditional news media because of the richness of their content. This is not to suggest that everything candidates claim on their sites is factually accurate or objectively true. Far from it. It simply means that Web sites offer a vastly greater volume of political—and politicized—information than is contained in television ads or print advertising. Even a citizen who follows a campaign by reading newspapers closely would require a good deal of time and effort to obtain a volume of information about any particular candidate comparable to what is available at the average Web site. If a citizen comes away from a Web site having acquired new information or beliefs of any kind, we consider that an increase in knowledge in the most basic sense.

We expect changes in feelings toward candidates to be coupled tightly to changes in knowledge. Political audiences are likely to seek out and believe information that is consistent with their prior beliefs, while avoiding and disbelieving information that is not. This should reinforce their positive feelings toward the candidate. On the whole, citizens should leave a Web site both better informed *and* more positive about the candidate they preferred than when they first arrived at the home page.

A third level of the possible effects of Web sites is ultimately the most important: influencing political behavior, especially voting. As we saw in chapter 3, campaigns make a concerted effort to turn supporters visiting their Web sites into volunteers or donors and, of course, to motivate them to act on their preferences by turning out on election day. Indeed, the other possible influences of Web sites on their audiences are really just a prelude to this ultimate goal of stimulating people to act in a way favorable to the candidates.

These three levels of influence—from stimulating return visits to motivating action—have increasing potential consequences then. At-

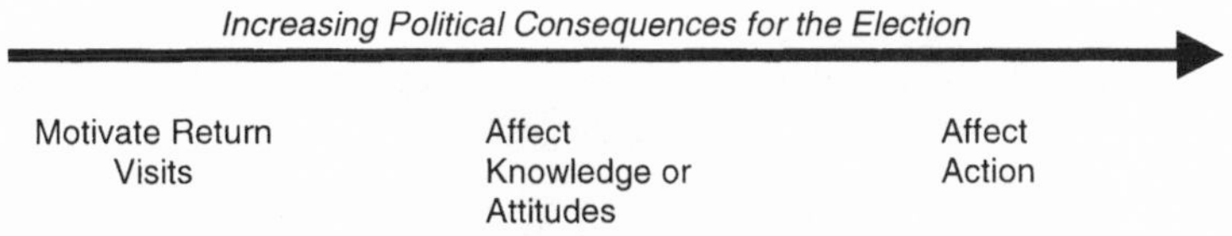

| Motivate Return Visits | Affect Knowledge or Attitudes | Affect Action |

Figure 5.1. Schematic hierarchy of Web site effects on citizens

tracting voters back to the site and strengthening their feelings of support and their knowledge are fine, but none of that matters if the candidate's efforts online do not produce political action of some kind by the voter. These actions are represented graphically in figure 5.1, organized from least to most significant politically.[1]

Motivating Return Visits

We begin at the left end of the scale in figure 5.1, with motivating return visits. While we expected to find that a substantial number of people returned to candidate Web sites after their initial visit, we were surprised at how large the number really was. Overall, slightly more than half of the people in our national survey (55 percent) who visited at least one site one time reported they had made two or more visits to a particular Web site. Among the candidate sites, the Bush campaign's attracted the largest fraction of returning visitors at 57 percent, while Nader's and Buchanan's attracted the fewest at under 40 percent. Table 5.1 shows the figures for each site. These numbers may somewhat underestimate the fraction of people who only make one visit, because of recall effects. People who visited a site more than once are more likely than one-time visitors to recall the visit when asked in a survey, even during the heat of the campaign when much of the audience would have seen a site relatively recently.

Still, two conclusions can be drawn. For a substantial fraction of the audience for Web sites, the experience is more than a curiosity and one-time experience. Second, the interest in returning varies substantially across the various site-audience combinations.

At the state level, the pattern is again similar with the high-profile Senate race resembling the major-party presidential race and the gov-

127

Table 5.1.

Fraction of each site's audience that made at least one return visit

Bush audience	57%
Gore audience	48%
Nader audience	39%
Buchanan audience	37%
Nonpartisan site audience	41%
Combined audiences	55%

Notes: Source is authors' national Web audience survey. N=979.

ernor's race resembling more the dynamics of the presidential minor-party candidates. About 45 percent of the Ashcroft audience and 49 percent of the Carnahan audience made more than one visit to the candidate's site, but for both Holden and Talent the figure was about 25 percent.

Though the evidence does not provide direct confirmation, the reason for this difference may have been initially identified by the campaign staffs: mass media coverage of candidates running for office is an important stimulator of visits to Web sites. We hypothesize that supporters of a candidate are more likely to make return visits to a Web site when their attention is directed to the candidate and the race by the mass media. We interpret this as an indicator of a larger phenomenon of vital importance to online campaigning: Voters' interactions with "new" media are heavily conditioned by what happens in the "old," traditional media of television and print news. Because of the overwhelming capacity of traditional mass media to direct voters' attention, campaign Web sites remain dependent to a substantial degree on the mass media.

What distinguishes these return visitors from people who visit a campaign Web site once and then never return? Is it level of education, age, gender, race, partisanship, ideology, or political knowledge?

In general, three factors make a difference: education, political knowledge, and partisanship.[2] About 63 percent of people with a col-

lege degree who visited any of the sites in our survey went back subsequently, compared with 49 percent of those without a college degree.[3] Return visitors also were slightly more knowledgeable about
politics.[4] On top of the fact that the demographics of Internet users
are skewed toward higher socioeconomic status, Web sites tend to
attract the better educated and more knowledgeable from among the
population of Internet users. Since about one-quarter of American
adults beyond college age have a bachelor's degree, this core audience
of return visitors to Web sites is more than twice as likely as randomly
chosen citizens to have completed four years of college.

As for partisanship, Republicans and Democrats were more
likely in general to return to Web sites than were independents, with
Republicans favoring George Bush's site and Democrats Al Gore's.
About 56 percent of partisans returned, compared with only 46 percent of independents. And the stronger were people's partisan identification, the more likely they were to make return visits, as figure
5.2 shows.

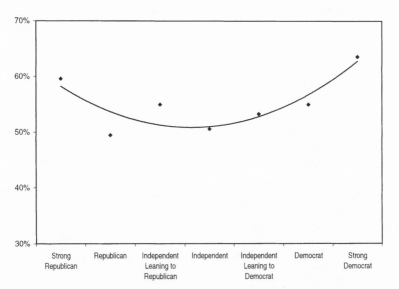

Figure 5.2. Effect of partisanship on repeat visits to presidential Web sites. The data show the percentage of each category of Web site audience that made more than one visit. Data for all Web sites
combined. $R^2=0.75$; N=1,008.

The reasons that people return to a Web site are revealing. Across all of the candidates' sites, far and away the most common reason for return visits was to "learn about issues." While this goal was also important in motivating first visits, as we saw in the previous chapter, it competed with "just browsing" and a combination of other factors. For repeat visitors, issues easily rise to the fore. Roughly speaking, about half of return visits are motivated by an interest in issue information, while the other half are divided among a half dozen or so motivations. We were particularly interested to note how unimportant were features of the site design. Table 5.2 shows the frequency with which our survey respondents mentioned each of eight reasons for a return visit.

Together, these findings round out the dynamics of return visits. Repeat visitors are knowledgeable, well-educated, partisan, and seeking more issue information in support of their political preferences. They return not because they are trying to decide whom to vote for or to learn more about the candidate, but apparently because they enjoy the political information and content that they find online, and also because they like to follow news of the campaign.

Table 5.2.
Main reason for returning to a candidate's campaign site

	Bush	Gore	Nader	Buchanan
Just to browse with no specific purpose in mind	19%	19%	14%	25%
Learning about the candidate's issue positions	50%	49%	58%	51%
In order to obtain general information about the campaign	0%	0%	0%	0%
Because I like the candidate or party	0%	0%	0%	0%
Learning about the candidate as an individual	7%	8%	3%	0%
Because of the design of the site or some unique feature of its content	2%	2%	0%	0%
Obtaining news about the candidate	20%	20%	24%	24%
Donating or volunteering	3%	3%	1%	0%

Notes: Figures show the fractions of visitors to the candidates' Web sites offering each purpose as the primary reason they returned to the sites. Source is authors' national Web audience survey. For Bush, N=289; for Gore, N=187; for Nader, N=62; for Buchanan, N=19. Statistical significance varies.

Knowledge and Feeling Effects

One of the most important questions about media exposure is: How much do people learn from it? This question is vital in a political campaign as candidates spend tens of millions of dollars on advertising to educate voters about themselves.

This question logically can be extended to the Internet. Do people learn from being exposed to election Web sites? Are they better informed about the campaign (for example, who is running, some candidate background information, when the election is held, and so forth) because of the Internet?[5]

The answer is yes and no. At the national level, exposure to Web sites made a small difference for a minority of people. Overall, about 19 percent of research subjects in our laboratory settings increased their level of political knowledge by viewing candidate Web sites.[6]

The outcomes for the Missouri races were somewhat different, however. About 57 percent of subjects in the experiment—three times the national average—who saw the state-level sites improved their knowledge of the candidates.[7] The disparity between the two levels likely is due to the comparatively lower level of media coverage of state-level races. People knew less about statewide races, therefore their information levels easily could increase by exposure to candidate Web sites in a research setting. By recruiting a random group of adults into a laboratory setting and directing them to look at particular Web sites, we were in effect playing the role of mass media in directing their attention. Unlike mass media, however, we gave equal time to all candidates.

In order to tap into people's disparate interests and to accommodate the fact that what people learned at sites likely varied substantially as a function of prior interest, we asked people about their perceptions of whether they learned from the sites, regardless of the content. Of course, such self-reported measures are open to misperception, but we still found it valuable to discover whether people thought they learned anything. To a large degree, people's attitudes about politics, their preferences among candidates, and their inclinations to vote are a function of subjective perceptions and beliefs, right or wrong. Whether people are well informed in an objective sense is often less important in influencing behavior than whether they feel informed. For this reason, we asked people whether they had learned anything from the site. We differentiated learning about candidates as individuals from learning about candidates' positions on issues.

The results are generally consistent with our simple objective test. For the Bush and Gore audiences, roughly comparable fractions—about one-third—of people reported that they learned something new about the candidate as a person or about the candidate's position on issues. In the case of the Bush site, about 34 percent of our subjects reported that they learned something new about his issue positions, while 32 percent reported learning about him as an individual—a statistically indistinguishable difference in a sample of this size. For Gore, slightly fewer people (27 percent) reported learning about issue positions, but a comparable number (32 percent) learned about the candidate as an individual. For the minor-party candidates, the results were different: Substantially more people reported learning about the candidate's issue positions than among the Gore and Bush audiences—57 percent in the case of Nader and 43 percent in the case of Buchanan.

This complements our survey findings about the greater role played by issue information than by candidate information for Web site audiences. It also provides circumstantial evidence that the mass media leave citizens especially uninformed about the issue positions of minor-party candidates. The tendency of traditional media to focus on personality and the campaign horse race certainly affects all candidates, but it appears especially likely to leave citizens in the dark about issues where minor-party candidates are concerned. We find it especially intriguing that our subjects were less likely to learn from the Web information about Nader and Buchanan as people and substantially more likely to come away with new information about their issue positions.

The situation in the Missouri races was somewhat more complex. Larger fractions of our research subjects who saw the Missouri sites than those who saw a presidential site reported that they learned something. This was true for learning both about issues and about the candidates as people. Roughly half of the Missouri audience in the experiment reported learning more about the candidates' issue positions, which is substantially more than the third or so of the presidential audience who felt they learned about issues.

This supports our general conclusion that patterns of media coverage of candidates establish a baseline level of knowledge among voters and thereby influence their comparative levels of demand for additional information about issues and candidates through the Web. Yet the Missouri audience showed an even greater responsiveness to candidate information than to issue information, unlike the national audience. On average, nearly three-quarters of the Missouri audience members reported that they learned something about Ashcroft, Carnahan, Holden, or Talent as individuals, compared with less than a third of the national audience members who reported learning about at least one of the presidential candidates. This is the reverse of the national pattern in which learning about issues outpaced learning about individuals. A summary of these figures is shown in table 5.3.

The evidence from our experiment is only tentative, but we suggest the following as the most plausible interpretation of this finding. Since the Missouri statewide races received minimal news coverage through most of the election year, the amount of candidate information that voters were receiving was limited. Hence, the baseline for information concerning these candidates was lower than for presidential candidates, who receive extensive coverage via both news media

Table 5.3.
Self-perception of learning from candidate Web sites

	Learned about Candidate's Issue Positions	Learned about Candidate as a Person
Presidential candidates		
Bush	34%	32%
Gore	27%	32%
Nader	57%	28%
Buchanan	43%	25%
State candidates		
Ashcroft	47%	97%
Carnahan	63%	73%
Holden	40%	80%
Talent	48%	43%

Notes: Source is authors' experimental data. N=210. Statistical significance varies.

and paid advertising. When interested, engaged voters (such as those who visit Web sites) are presented a choice among candidates about whom they receive comparatively little information from mass media coverage, as in the case of state-level candidates such as Talent and Holden, but also even figures like Ashcroft and Carnahan, they exhibit a relatively high demand for information first about the candidates as individuals and second about the candidates' issue positions. When presented a choice among candidates about whom they receive comparatively large amounts of information from mass media coverage, as in the case of Bush and Gore, they exhibit a relatively high demand for issue information first and personal information second, though in both cases this demand is lighter than in the case of lesser-known candidates. This general thesis accounts for most of the differences we found between the two general classes of candidates: major-party presidential candidates and minor-party presidential candidates along with state-level candidates. Yet patterns of differences among state-level candidates themselves and between minor-party presidential candidates and state candidates remain to be explained. Our research was not designed to tease out such differences, but they may be important.

Changes in feelings toward candidates should be connected to knowledge effects. Those least likely to actually change their viewpoints on candidates would be those with the greatest knowledge and interest in politics, while those most likely simply to learn something new would be those with less knowledge. In the realm of mass media, research by John Zaller and others has shown that people who are *moderately* aware of politics are more likely to be influenced by campaign communication and news than either highly aware people or the unaware.[8] Highly aware citizens are most likely to be exposed to traditional campaign communications and news, but quite unlikely to be persuaded to change their views by anything they see.

On the other hand, highly unaware citizens, who potentially stand to gain the most in the way of new information that might be persuasive, are least likely to be exposed to it in the first place. This leaves the middle range of citizens susceptible to both exposure to information and persuasion by it. This principle applies with a twist to the Internet, because of the intentionality involved in viewing campaign sites. People unaware of politics and disinterested do not tend to visit political Web sites, as we saw in the last chapter. This fact truncates the mass media audience, leaving those who tend toward moderate to high levels of political awareness and engagement.

Do people change their feelings about a candidate after seeing the candidate's Web site? For example, one might expect people who opposed a candidate to become less hostile after exposure to a Web site, or at least candidates would hope so. Is this true?[9]

Among the small fraction of people in our survey who opposed the candidate whose site they saw, people reported to us that the Web sites had essentially no effect on whether they supported the candidate. About 10 percent of visitors to the Bush site were opponents, and the figure remained unchanged after they visited the site. Gore's site drew more opponents, about 20 percent, and this figure also was unaffected.

Two of the sites did produce very modest effects on the minority of visitors who were undecided. This effect was strongest at the Nader site. Nader's Web audience was evenly divided between supporters and neutral citizens at about 47 percent each before the first visit. About a third of the neutral audience reported to us that after their visit they felt supportive of Nader. Bush experienced a much more modest effect; about a quarter of the neutral visitors reported feeling supportive of Bush after their first visit. For both candidates, this effect was concentrated among men. For Bush, it also was concentrated among ideological moderates, and for Nader it was concentrated among those without a college education.

On a scale ranging from "liking the candidate a lot more" to "disliking the candidate a lot more," about 60 percent said they felt no differently about the candidate, with the remainder more likely to report feeling more positive about the candidate than more negative. Figure 5.3 organizes the combined audiences for the four presidential Web sites by their responses to the sites, from those reporting that their experience made them like the candidates a lot more to those saying the experience made them dislike the candidates a lot more, with three categories between these endpoints.

The curve shows that Web sites seem to have no effect on most citizens, while exerting a more positive than negative effect on the rest.

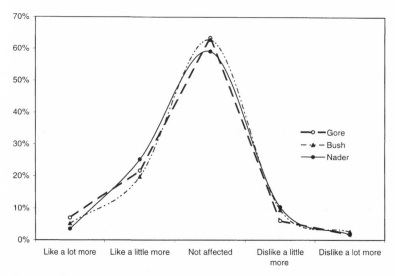

Figure 5.3. Effects of presidential Web sites on feelings toward candidates. The lines show the fraction of each Web site's audience that reported the site affected their feelings as shown on the horizontal axis. Source is authors' national Web audience survey. N=979.

On average, about 25–30 percent of each site's audience reported feeling either a little or a lot more positive about the candidate, while less than half that number reported liking the candidate a little or a lot less. When combined with the fact that the audiences are predominantly supporters to begin with, this finding shows polarization of the public at work.

In our experimental data, we approached the measurement of feelings differently, but found similar results. Rather than asking people to tell us whether the Web site affected how they felt, we simply asked them at the outset how strongly they felt about each candidate, then exposed them to the candidate's Web site, and afterward asked them again how strongly they felt. By comparing their before and after answers, we were able to make our own direct inferences about the effects of the site on feelings. Again, we found that most people were not affected, with a larger minority ending up reinforced in their feelings and a smaller minority experiencing a shift in the other direction.

The most important finding about feeling effects to come out of the laboratory experiments is an interaction between liking a candidate and learning from the candidate's Web site. People who came away from a candidate's Web site liking him more or less were also people who came away having learned something. And the liking-learning relationship is exclusively associated with learning about issue positions. Learning personal information about the candidate as an individual bore no relationship to liking him more or less as a candidate. For instance, in the case of Nader's site, 72 percent of people who reported that they liked the candidate more or less as a result of visiting his Web site also told us that they learned something about his issue positions, compared with 47 percent of people whose feelings about Nader were unaffected.[10] There were no statistically significant differences among those whose feelings changed as to whether they learned personal information about Nader. The effect was similar for Buchanan, where 60 percent of those whose feelings were affected learned about issues, compared with 29 percent whose feelings were not, and again there was no effect as a result of learning about Buchanan as an individual.[11]

The effect was somewhat weaker for Bush and Gore. For Bush, 53 percent of those whose feelings changed had learned about issues, compared with 23 percent of those whose feelings did not, and again there were no differences on the measure of learning about Bush as an individual.[12] This effect appeared also in the case of the Gore Web site, but it did not reach statistical significance.

These relationships represent correlations, not necessarily causal connections. We cannot say for sure whether changes in feelings toward the candidate lead to learning, or whether the process works the other way around. Untangling that tightly coupled relationship with systematic evidence is beyond the scope of this study, but we surmise that most likely the relationship works in both directions. The more people like a candidate, the more likely they are to learn about him, and as they learn, their feelings toward the candidate are likely to strengthen. At the very least, the two changes in people's minds are inextricably linked.

Effects on Voting

The possibility that Web sites might have effects on political actions and behavior is of course the ultimate test of their consequence in politics. Therefore the most important question would be: What effect do Web sites have on voter turnout and vote choice?[13]

Campaign site visitors are well above the national average in their tendency to vote. Of those who saw a campaign Web site, 91 percent reported that they were "very likely" to vote, compared with 73 percent of those who did not see a campaign site. When we resurveyed 300 members of the Web audience three months after the election, we found that 84 percent of the people who had told us earlier that they had seen a campaign Web site reported that they had in fact voted. This is a very high number, since nationwide turnout in the election was only about 50 percent, but it is consistent with what people had told us earlier about their intentions.[14]

The most plausible reason, of course, for high turnout comes from what we know about the Web audience's background: They were more interested, knowledgeable, and committed to candidates than others even before they saw a campaign Web site. But it is also logically possible that they were more likely to vote *because* they saw a Web site, or at least that their already high likelihood of voting was increased even further by their experiences at a Web site. Understanding these two possibilities is a major objective of people involved in online campaigning, and it can be approached only indirectly.

Our best approach was to examine the people in our first survey wave who told us that their Web experience had made them more likely to vote. This included about 49 percent of visitors to the Bush site and 35 percent of visitors to the Gore site. It is interesting to note, by the way, that the smaller effect of the Gore site is accounted for entirely by men, only 28 percent of whom reported an increased interest in voting. The Gore figure for women was 48 percent, indistinguishable statistically from the Bush numbers for men and women. This was yet another indicator in our data that women responded much more positively to the Gore site than did men. In our second survey wave of the same people, we compared these enthusiasts' actual

138

reports of voting to the voting reports of people who had not told us that the Web made any difference.

What we found is the complete absence of any difference in voting rates between the two groups. For both the Bush and Gore sites, there was no relationship between reported responses to the Web site prior to the election and actual reports of voting after the election.[15]

This conclusion is generally consistent with what people told us about the Internet experience when we asked them to look back on it after the election. In our panel immediately after the election and again in the panel three months later, few respondents had anything positive to say about the helpfulness of the Web sites or the Internet more generally in reaching a voting decision. For instance, in the immediate postelection panel, about 12 percent of the Web audience reported that a campaign site had been helpful to them, compared with 65 percent who reported that newspapers or television had been helpful, but many could not even remember having visited a Web site. In the three-month panel, only 16 percent of people who had earlier told us they had seen Bush's Web site still recalled having done so, along with 12 percent of the Gore audience. While data such as these cannot establish conclusively that the Web had no effect on turnout, they provide a strongly suggestive case, especially when viewed in light of all the other findings about who visits Web sites and why.

Accepting the conclusion that there is little reason to think candidate Web sites affected overall turnout, the final remaining question concerns vote choice. Is it possible that the Web affected which candidates citizens voted for, even if it did not stimulate turnout?

The answer here is likely to be "no," though we cannot say with certainty. Since most people visit sites of their preferred candidate, and since for the most part Web sites either exert no effect on feelings or strengthen positive feelings, there is little room for people to make up their minds or even to change them. Still, nontrivial minorities of the visitors to Web sites were undecided or opposed, and so the effects on these voters should be considered.

To do this, we examined people who ended up voting for someone other than the candidate they told us they had preferred in our first wave. These voters amounted to only 4 percent of the participants in the panel survey, 12 out of 300. We used a multivariate statistical technique to examine the characteristics of this 4 percent of citizens to see how they might differ from the much larger number whose vote was consistent with their intentions prior to the election.

What we found is that these vote switchers were no different than consistent voters in age, education, gender, political knowledge, partisan identification, attention to the campaigns on television, or experiences at the Web sites—with one exception that we will discuss shortly.[16] This means that none of the standard demographic characteristics predicted a change in vote, and apparently neither did the experience of visiting campaign Web sites. This test does not conclusively rule out the possibility that Web sites influenced people to change their votes, but it suggests that no obvious, straightforward relationship exists.

The 4 percent of vote switchers are interesting. They were substantially more likely to have seen the Nader Web site than people who did not switch their allegiance. The voters who changed their minds included a disproportionate number who told us at first that they intended to vote for Nader but who ended up voting for Gore. (Nader supporters switching to Bush and Gore supporters switching to Nader were negligible in our sample of Web audience members.) We cannot necessarily make the inference that the site actually *persuaded* people to vote for Gore. The more likely scenario is that people who preferred Nader but were unsure whether to vote for him or Gore were especially likely to visit the Nader site in the first place, and for any of a number of reasons—not necessarily connected to the Web site—they eventually voted for Gore.

This unusual twist of the 2000 election aside, we can find no evidence that the Web experiences at other candidate sites had any bearing on vote choice. It is clear that the citizens interested in the campaigns derived a measure of satisfaction and enjoyment from viewing the Web sites of their favored candidates, and they often felt reinforced in their political preferences. However, this enthusiasm did not translate into meaningful changes in likelihood of voting or in candidate preference. This means that as we investigated the spectrum of consequences of Web-based political communication from motivating a return visit to affecting voter turnout or even vote choice, we found

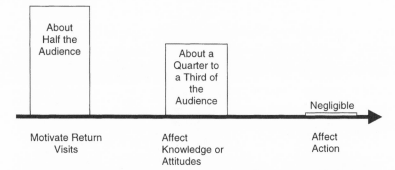

Figure 5.4. Schematic representation of incidence of presidential Web site effects on citizens

that the frequency of effects diminished rapidly. While about half of the Web audience was motivated to return for a subsequent visit, only about a quarter to a third learned something new or altered their feelings toward the candidates, and a negligible number, if any, were affected in their concrete decisions on whether to vote and whom to support. This pattern is shown in figure 5.4.

The fact that this survey research did not produce evidence of an effect of Web sites on voter turnout or vote choice is far from the last word on the subject. Attempting to identify a concrete consequence for human behavior from an event like visiting a Web site, as we have attempted here, is fraught with difficulties. The experiences of many years of research by scholars examining the influence of television on elections has shown that, in some campaigns, media effects are much more apparent and direct than in others, and they are in every case a challenge to measure reliably. Even assuming nothing more than that the Internet represents a new medium alongside television and newspapers would lead one to expect that the effects of the Internet would not necessarily be obvious in measures of turnout and vote choice. If Web sites really were to influence how or whether people vote, the effect would likely be very small and hard to detect at best. Still, we have found a good deal of evidence—all pointing in the same direction—in this and the previous chapter. Powerful limits exist on the capacity of campaign Web sites to alter people's intended behavior.

141

Reinforcement

We began with two basic questions: How do candidates use the Internet to communicate with voters? Do these messages reinforce or alter the attitudes and behavior of voters?

The evidence from our interviews, our analyses of Web site content, our surveys, and our laboratory experiments across the country provide some answers to these questions. At this point, we need to reiterate those answers and provide an interpretation.

Our first question is answered simply: Candidates clearly are incorporating the Internet into campaigns. Web sites are standard in candidate campaigns for federal or statewide office. In addition, candidates are employing e-mail communication to reach those voters who may not visit their sites. But Web sites and e-mail communication serve as supplemental tools rather than as replacements for traditional campaigning. The effect is an integrative one: Campaigns fold the Internet's functions into traditional campaign activities. For example, site visitors are encouraged to volunteer online, but what they are volunteering for are traditional campaign outreach efforts. Another example is use of the Web site or e-mail to perform the traditional campaign activity of informing journalists about campaign events and seeking to develop a positive media portrayal for the candidate.

Online communication has not replaced candidates' traditional activities of press relations, fundraising, speeches and rallies, and so forth. Specifically, candidates do not bypass the press in order to reach the voters. The relatively narrow reach of their Web sites compared with the size of the electorate necessitates prime dependence on the traditional means of voter communication. Hence, candidates' reliance on traditional paid media advertising continues even in the Internet age.

In terms of the online content of their messages, campaigns have homed in on the task of reinforcement. The primary intended audience consists of supporters, who need to be reinforced in their choice and mobilized to action on behalf of the campaign. Although those who are undecided or who oppose the candidate may constitute a minority of the audience, they are not the objects of the campaign's attention in its online presentation. Supporters are. Supporters receive messages to stick with the candidate, to become active in the campaign, and to turn out to vote (along with supportive family and friends) on election day. The main message of candidate Web content is reinforcement.

The answer to the second question is somewhat more complex. Are voters affected by campaign Web sites? It depends on the type of voter. For undecided voters, the effects are minimal. The candidate site audience overwhelmingly consists of those who have already decided whom they will vote for, rather than undecided voters who might be swayed by Web site content. Most undecided voters are not in a position to be influenced by Web sites—a message that campaign staffs may not want to hear. But the reality is not only that campaign sites fail to change the minds of citizens, but they also fail even to assist many undecided citizens in making up their minds.

But if our subject is the person who intends to vote for the candidate, then effects are more apparent. Supporters are far more likely than others to visit a candidate Web site. Once there, they are likely to return, and a small but nontrivial number end up knowing more about the candidate or feeling even more supportive, though these effects did not result in any change in voting behavior that we could

144

detect in 2000. Put simply, campaign Web sites attract supporters of the candidates who display them, and the messages of these sites have a modest tendency to strengthen and reinforce voters' predispositions.

Interpreting the Findings Theoretically

How can one make sense of these conclusions? Why do such strong limits seem to exist on the capacity of Web-based messages to alter political behavior?

One of the major objectives of a campaign for political office is directing public attention. In a campaign, a candidate seeks to focus voters' attention in a way that helps, for instance, on issues where the candidate is strong and the opponent weak. For example, in the 2000 campaign, the Gore campaign sought to emphasize the booming economy, while the Bush campaign raised matters of character. Candidates seek to use the agenda-setting power of whatever media are available to them to influence the issues to which citizens pay attention.[1] Without necessarily influencing *what* citizens think regarding any particular issue or what positions they take, media messages can influence *which* issues citizens think about. By emphasizing issues such as violent crime or the environment, journalists, candidates, and other elites direct citizens to think about these as important problems of the day, even if no particular citizen's views about gun control or clean air regulations or other policy questions are changed by the messages.

A related process is *priming*.[2] This refers to the ability of media messages to influence which issues or criteria citizens have in mind when they evaluate candidates and make choices. Again without necessarily influencing what citizens feel about any particular issue, media messages can direct citizens' attention from one issue to another, to the advantage of some candidates and the disadvantage of others. One of the classic instances of priming involves racial attitudes. For instance, in the 2000 campaign, by including black actors in a campaign advertisement attacking "wasteful" spending on government programs, the Bush campaign was able successfully to stimulate people to think in racial terms and draw upon their racial stereotypes in evaluating his candidacy and that of Al Gore.[3]

145

Another important way in which messages from candidates, journalists, and others influence the public's attention is by delivering messages that citizens are not necessarily seeking or expecting. The televised campaign advertisement is the ultimate form of this unsolicited, unexpected message. By catching citizens who are watching a favored television show, interrupting them, and delivering a political message, these ads have the potential to influence the public's political attention in one way or another. Television news has a similar effect, though not as stark. Citizens who sit down to watch the evening news are prepared to be informed or entertained, but they do not know just what messages they will be receiving. The reading of newspapers is similar, though it affords citizens a greater measure of control. Influences on public exposure and attention work best when the audience is large and captive.

This brings us to the Internet, which provides an audience that is increasingly large but far from captive. Viewing a Web site is not like viewing a campaign ad or even a televised news program, because the audience for any particular Web site must make an intentional choice to be exposed to the information contained there. The visitor to a Web site must take several active steps to view that message, including getting online, locating the political Web site among the millions of online choices, and then searching for the information at the Web site. In contrast, television viewers turn a dial or push a button and are fed a stream of information chosen for them by others.

This choice to be exposed to the political message is even more powerful than it is for television, radio, or newspapers because of the breadth of other viewing options available. For example, while television viewers have sometimes several hundred options for viewing, Internet users have millions of options. People who see the Web site of a candidate are therefore qualitatively different from people who might see a televised advertisement from that candidate because they have made a greater effort to view political information and have chosen such information from a wide array of alternative and probably more entertaining options. Aside from likely differences in socioeconomic status, the audiences for traditional media are more susceptible to unintentional exposure and potential influence.

CAMPAIGNING ONLINE Reinforcement

The Internet has real limitations with respect to influencing voters' attention. Candidates for office, campaign advisors, communications directors, and political party leaders are well aware that for all the wonders of interactivity and information intensiveness of the Internet, traditional mass media simply afford vastly greater opportunities to attract the public's attention. To be sure, opportunities for influencing public attention exist on the Internet, but these are dwarfed by the capacities of the mass media and its enormous and unsuspecting audiences.

The Internet cannot at present do what television and newspapers can: saturate a large audience with messages that interrupt citizens' focus and direct it toward the campaign and, more specifically, a candidate's message. The technology for something akin to this kind of interruption exists in the form of pop-up advertisements on the Internet, but these so far have failed to approach even remotely the power of broadcast advertisements, in large part because Internet advertising is so easily ignored by the audience. The mass audience for political advertising in traditional media is inadvertent, in this sense. Broadcast advertising is especially inadvertent, designed as it is to catch citizens in an unsuspecting state—while they are enjoying a favorite television comedy, perhaps—and then to disseminate political messages. Even television news has a comparatively high degree of inadvertency. Citizens who set out to watch the evening news may indeed seek information about public affairs, and perhaps even specific political news, but what they actually receive is a menu of political communications chosen very carefully for them by those in the broadcast business and their advertisers. This fact gives the mass media a capacity to direct public attention that does not exist on the Internet.

Another reason that limits exist on the capacity of campaign sites to alter behavior involves the tendency of voters to filter the messages with which they are bombarded, particularly those that are political. This tendency goes to the heart of how people navigate electoral campaigns. Unfortunately, citizens are often held to unrealistic expectations, especially in relation to voting. A common ideal of good citizenship holds that voters ought to study issues and candidates carefully, making ready for election day almost like students preparing for an exam. According to this ideal, discharging one's obligations as a voter entails being both informed and engaged. Yet, voters clearly fail to live up to the ideal. Many citizens routinely fail quizzes of political knowledge. They possess limited awareness about a range of current issues. As a result, it is common to lament their failures.

The problem with this lamentation lies in the ideal itself. Not only is it unreasonable to expect that people behave like philosopher-citizens—as it is unreasonable to expect that their leaders act like philosopher-kings—it is historically blind. As scholar Michael Schudson has shown, American citizens in practice have never approached this ideal, even in the halcyon days of the founding. For all of the romanticism with which Americans often look back on citizens of the late eighteenth and early nineteenth centuries, the fact is that the bulk of the citizenry was illiterate, uneducated, and vastly less well informed about affairs of state than modern citizens. The last thing that those who charge voters with ignorance would want would be a return to the state of preindustrial citizenship.

Nor has the task of following public affairs become any easier since then. As long ago as the early 1900s, Walter Lippmann argued persuasively that the complexity of modern life had reached such an advanced state that no voter could realistically dedicate sufficient time and energy to being well and broadly informed.[4] The increasing complexity and interconnection of public life since Lippmann's time, along with the dramatically expanded volume of communication and information, means that voters are even less well positioned than at the end of the Progressive Era to fulfill a Jeffersonian ideal of knowledge and engagement.

Theories of voter selectivity, which come mainly from the study of political psychology, provide by far the most helpful and powerful way of understanding how people respond to this situation and why they behave as they do on the Internet.[5] Selectivity refers to the powerful tendency people exhibit to seek and to believe information that reinforces their existing beliefs and predispositions. People's interactions with the many streams of communication and information that surround them in the mass media, their workplaces, their communities, and even their networks of friends and associates exhibit this selectivity. In public life, people tend to seek out sources of information likely to confirm their existing beliefs, rather than seeking a balanced set of information and then weighing the evidence in both directions.[6] In short, liberals like to get their information from liberal sources and conservatives from conservative sources.

The term *selective exposure* is most often used to describe this process. People seek out information consistent with both their ideology and their partisanship. Shanto Iyengar, Kyu Hahn, and Markus Prior have also shown that people are selective with respect to issues of interest to them. Not surprisingly, people pay closest attention to those issues that bear more directly on their own lives, and they tend to ignore issues that resonate less closely with their own interests. When combined with ideological and partisan filtering of information, this means that among the vast array of information and political communication available to voters, each tends to pay the closest attention to just that information that confirms what they already believe about the issues of closest interest to them.[7]

Selective acceptance takes this tendency even further. When exposed inadvertently to information that is inconsistent with prior beliefs and values, citizens are especially likely to reject it as false. Charles Tabor and Milton Lodge call this "motivated skepticism," showing that people tend to accept at face value political communication and information that confirms their prior beliefs and partisan dispositions, while being highly skeptical and even dismissive of information that disconfirms their existing beliefs.[8] A tendency even exists to perceive objectively balanced news sources as biased in favor of positions with which one disagrees, simply because the news is not biased obviously toward one's own favored position.[9] All of these effects mean that in influencing what people accept as true and what they reject, the most relevant factor is the previous political orientation of the individual.

This kind of selectivity appears in a variety of contexts. For instance, it has been shown to be especially strong at the interpersonal level. Research confirms the intuitive observation that people tend to associate with others who share their viewpoints. Moreover, people are most likely to discuss with their friends and associates those political issues and topics where they have the greatest overlap and consistency in beliefs.[10] It also appears in highly impersonal contexts, such as the ways that people react to televised political advertisements. Stephen Ansolabehere and Shanto Iyengar show that the impact of advertisements is powerfully conditioned by voters' interests, beliefs, and partisan predispositions. Specifically, their impact is a function of how ads "resonate" with those prior predispositions. This means that advertising leads to very little crossover voting; instead, it tends to reinforce prior beliefs. In general, political campaigns tend to exacerbate differences in political knowledge. The energies of candidates and the media to inform and persuade the public mean that, in the end, people who are well informed become even more so.[11]

Just why people's thinking about politics is so highly biased and contingent on prior beliefs is not clear. From a simplistic perspective, people seem "irrational" when they cling to past beliefs in the face of new information, and it might appear puzzling why this would be the case. Yet, from a more subtle perspective, people's selectivity may be perfectly reasonable and adaptive in the context of an environment rich in information and stimuli. When the volume of information and communication directed at people through their social and media environments vastly exceeds any person's capacity to absorb and weigh carefully, the most reasonable and "rational" strategy may simply be to cling to past beliefs except under truly extraordinary circumstances.[12] Michael MacKuen, W. Russell Neuman, and George E. Marcus refer to this phenomenon as "affective political intelligence." They suggest that emotional dispositions form the baseline human orientation in politics and that it is best for voters to reassess and reconsider those dispositions, in light of new information, only infrequently.[13]

So, to say that humans are selective thinkers or are "biased" in what they learn is not necessarily to say that they are irrational or illogical. The vast array of information and communication directed at citizens certainly exceeds by a wide margin what anyone could reasonably absorb and evaluate in a balanced, objective manner. The most efficient approach for an individual in that kind of environment—and, in that sense, the most evolutionarily rational—may be to follow the simple rule of always favoring one's own prior beliefs about the world and screening out most of what is occurring in one's environment.

We believe that our research on the Internet provides a vivid demonstration of how the same patterns of selectivity that people have exhibited in the world of traditional media have carried over into the world of the Internet. Indeed, the Internet appears to be the ultimate medium for eliciting selectivity of various kinds from citizens.

Compared with other sources of information, television news tends to provide little opportunity for selective exposure. By presenting large (and therefore heterogeneous) audiences with brief, entertainment-oriented, nonpartisan stories about public affairs, television permits comparatively little selectivity by voters.[14] Newspapers, on the other hand, appear to have the potential for greater selectivity. This effect has been demonstrated clearly in situations where citizens have available to them more than one local newspaper. Diana Mutz and Paul Martin show that, for both the United States and the United Kingdom, citizens who have more choices among newspapers are less likely to encounter information that disagrees with or disconfirms their prior beliefs and partisan orientations.[15] That is, give citizens two or more newspapers exhibiting some variation in editorial orientation, and people will read the paper that most closely matches their own orientation. The result is that people's reading of newspapers tends to reinforce their own interests and beliefs rather than changing or refining them.

For example, in the Washington, D.C., area, conservatives tend to subscribe to the *Washington Times* while liberals prefer the *Washington Post*. Compared with voters who have only one paper to read, voters with a choice between two newspapers will get a politically narrower diet of information. Counterintuitively, then, the greater control that voters have over what they see and the wider the choices of information sources that voters have, the more selective they will be and the narrower the range of political perspectives they will encounter.[16] What happens on the Internet is merely an extension of this process.[17]

In general, three factors can affect how much any particular medium facilitates selectivity by voters: volume, diversity, and control.

1. The greater the volume of political information to which voters are exposed, the greater the *need* for selectivity.
2. The greater the diversity of sources, the greater the *extent* of selectivity that is possible.

3. The greater the choice a medium provides to voters over what they see, hear, or read, the more *frequent* the opportunities for selectivity.[18]

Various media can be rated on these three criteria. Television news provides little volume, diversity, or control, while talk radio shows and, in many cases, newspapers provide somewhat more diversity and control, if not necessarily a greater volume of information. By these criteria, the Internet surpasses these other media easily. It provides an enormous volume of political information; it contains vast diversity of sources for that information; and it gives voters very high levels of control. Table 6.1 summarizes this comparison of the Internet and other media in general, theoretical terms. While our study was not designed to produce detailed data comparing television, newspapers, or radio talk shows with the Internet, we believe that our multiple sources of evidence about the Internet show clearly the effects of selectivity at work, and they strongly suggest that the Internet is the medium with the greatest potential for citizen selectivity yet. This characteristic lies at the heart of the Internet's consequences for democracy.

If there is a general rule about the consequences of campaigns on citizens that has been learned from decades of analysis during the age of television, it is that campaigns exacerbate differences in political knowledge among people. The limitations of the Internet compared with broadcast media to influence public attention, combined with selectivity, means that the Internet largely amplifies this effect. In doing so, it illuminates an important lesson about technology and human

Table 6.1.
Media and conditions for selectivity in voter learning

	Volume of Information	Diversity of Sources	Extent of Choice by Voters	Combined Potential for Selectivity
Television news	Low	Low	Low	Low
Newspapers	Medium	Low	Medium	Medium
Talk shows	Low	Medium	Low	Medium
World Wide Web	High	High	High	High

behavior in politics. Technological change creates new opportunities for human action. It permits citizens to do what they might not have been able to do before, but it hardly compels them to act in new ways. The choices they make and the patterns of behavior that emerge are the product of psychological habits and tendencies that are little affected by new technology.

In attempting to understand the consequences of new media for democracy, it is important to avoid the mistake of assuming that technology alters human psychology merely because it alters the material and informational environment of humanity. As Curtis Gans has noted: "While candidates and non-profit organizations may design the most complete sources of information and the most compelling presentations of that information, what they cannot do is provide the motivation to access those sites."[19]

Proponents of dramatic Internet effects on campaigns have assumed that the Internet's role, like television's role in the early 1960s, would increase as time passed. Through the elections of 1996, 1998, and even 2000, supporters waited for the contemporary version of the magic new media moment, such as the Kennedy-Nixon debate of 1960. It is plausible (if unprovable) to argue, as some do, that Nixon might have been elected in 1960 had television not existed, and it is clearly the case that the influence of television grew in the elections following that year. Therefore, some have argued, the influence of the Internet on campaigns in the contemporary period will grow over time. Sure, the skeptic might say, Internet effects from campaigning online are hard to pin down now, but just wait a few years.

This expectation is at best only half true. Candidates' organizations are certainly growing more sophisticated in their use of new media. And increasingly, Internet technologies and television technologies will integrate. Those developments may indeed accelerate changes in the relationships between the public and the candidates offering themselves for office and may enhance some effects of the Internet. On the other hand, the human predilection for selectivity in thinking and learning about politics will hardly be altered by advancing technology. Voters will continue to use the medium for their own purposes, one of which is assuring themselves that their prior beliefs and predispositions are correct ones.

153

This characteristic of the new media in campaigns can be best understood in terms of renewal versus reinforcement. Many people have looked at the Internet and imagined a renewal of citizen engagement with democracy. In this vision, citizens turned off from politics become re-engaged through new opportunities for learning and action during elections. Citizens uninformed about candidates feast on the informational bounty of the Internet.

The potential for improvement certainly does seem real. When tested in scientifically constructed surveys—and other settings—Americans demonstrate levels of knowledge about politics that seem shockingly low to most. A majority of citizens are unable to answer correctly even the most basic questions about their democracy. Studies since 1960 have shown, for example, that only 45 percent of Americans know that it is Congress that declares war; only 41 percent can define the Bill of Rights; only 36 percent can define *primary election;* only 35 percent know what the electoral college is; only 25 percent know the length of a senator's term; and only 20 percent can name any two First Amendment rights. Only 46 percent of Americans can name their incumbent congressional candidate; only 35 percent can name both of their U.S. senators; and only 28 percent can name their state senator.[20]

Among political professionals, this state of affairs can either be a source of nagging doubt about the health of the system in which they work, or an opportunity to be exploited under the right circumstances. Where elected officials strive in good faith to divine the wishes and interests of the public and to make policies that accord with them, the fact that so many citizens seem to know so little about what is happening around them is hardly a source of satisfaction to professionals. To spend months or years of effort negotiating a new law on behalf of constituents who cannot identify you by name is too often the norm in politics.

By the same token, the fact that so many citizens are not knowledgeable about decisions being made on their behalf can create a kind of political vacuum, a zone of autonomy for elected officials insofar as citizen-constituents are concerned. The players who step into this are organized political interests. Those with the resources and motivation to hire lobbyists and private representatives to do the work of

154

being knowledgeable and attentive to democratic affairs become the de facto constituents of elected officials.[21] Although we are aware of no survey that gauges how much each citizen believes other Americans know about politics, we would surmise that most people would be surprised at how little their fellow citizens know. That is, even the metaknowledge of the fact of most citizens' low levels of knowledge is something that likely escapes many people. So too does the fact that the cynicism that citizens feel toward the power of organized interests and the tendency of many people to withdraw from politics because government seems unduly influenced by organized groups actually adds fuel to the problem that concerns them.

Clearly, the evidence shows that a correction of such problems, a renewal, is not happening, and it really does not make sense to expect it when one considers how the dynamics of public attention and selectivity work. Instead of these effects, the Internet appears to have other consequences where campaigns for office are concerned: possibly buttressing tendencies to vote and to learn among the engaged, and fortifying partisan predispositions and candidate preferences. The Internet reinforces patterns of citizen engagement in elections rather than breaking down old patterns or renewing this aspect of citizenship.

The Internet's role in elections will be affected by changes in the demographics of Internet use. In other words, those who go online today do not share the level of political interest of those who have gone online in the past. The early Internet users, who became politically involved online in the mid-1990s, were especially likely to be not only registered voters but political sophisticates. This means that easily as late as 2000 and probably for several elections beyond, the population of Internet users was and will continue to be highly skewed toward unusually active citizens. But as online access goes more mainstream, those initial users are being overtaken numerically by people who are much less interested in political information.

According to a Pew survey at the time of the November 2000 election, those who had gone online for the first time in the previous six months were least likely of all online users to utilize the Internet for election news information. While one-third of those who had been online for more than three years used the Internet in that way, fewer than one in six of those who had gone online for the first time in the previous year did so.

Michael Cornfield argues that the real digital divide is between those who are active and those who are not. Whether they have access to the Internet matters less than whether they choose to participate. According to Cornfield, "For every likely voter willing to visit a campaign Web site, there are three to four others who won't. Millions of other Americans who use the Internet have little to no intention of voting, let alone looking into a campaign."[22] Echoing Cornfield's assessment, pollster Frank Luntz concluded that the problem with the Internet and politics is that "Americans don't like politics. So when they get on the Web, politics is the last thing they want to read."[23]

This avoidance of politics is symbolized in the demise of commercial online political information sites. Prominent political dot. coms, such as Voter.com, SpeakOut.com, and Grassroots.com, either have closed their doors or scrambled to stay afloat, typically by turning away from the goal of providing voter information toward the more commercially profitable business of offering services for online advocacy.

Another example is the public's reaction to online coverage of the 2000 conventions. These conventions were considered the first real online conventions. Online convention coverage reached a new peak with attention devoted by Internet companies and traditional news organizations utilizing the Internet for news dissemination. Yet, the audience for this Internet information was negligible. Only 10 percent of online users actually saw anything about the Republican convention. Of those, two-thirds said they spent only a few seconds a day looking at it. Only 15 percent of those who saw anything about the conventions said they spent more than 10 minutes viewing online information about the conventions.[24] Compared with the total electorate or even the number of those who watched the convention on television, exposure online was minuscule.

These figures point to the following important fact: The *fraction* of people with Internet access who use the new technology for political purposes is likely to shrink over time, until Internet diffusion stops. Certainly the absolute number of Americans who go online for election information is increasing. However, as a proportion of all users, the audience is vulnerable to decline as the tide of new "immigrants" into the world of the Internet is dominated by the politically disinterested. It is quite possible, then, that the reinforcement effects we have described in the 2000 election, which constitute the main effect of the Internet, will be confined to a proportionally smaller (though numerically larger) niche of the Internet in the future.

Three Effects among Engaged Citizens: Issues, Learning, and Minor Parties

To say that the Internet tends to reinforce patterns of engagement and citizenship in the domain of elections is not to say that the Internet has no measurable effects or that it is devoid of consequences altogether. When we examine the landscape of online campaigning for office, we see few signs of the undecided voter, let alone the nonvoter, but we do see some interesting and potentially significant effects involving the committed voter. In addition to the central tendency toward reinforcement, our research suggests three intriguing effects of online campaigns.

The first of these involves issues themselves. If all of the developments in American election campaigns over the last half century were to be distilled down to a single process, it would be the emergence and triumph of the candidate over the issue. Most national campaigns prior to the 1960s were contests between representatives of parties advocating one or another vision and package of policies or benefits to citizens. To be sure, candidates mattered, but they mattered most often in the context of these contests between parties advocating different platforms of promised action. Increasingly since the 1960s, campaigns have evolved into contests among candidates offering themselves first as individuals and second as representatives of parties and platforms of issue positions.

Candidate-centrism is most readily apparent in conflicts over the character of candidates, but it is far more pervasive and insidious than just explicit episodes of character politics. Every time a candidate for office focuses more on making an appearance on television and looking good for the camera than on offering a thoughtful discussion of how to solve a public problem and every time the voter responds to this focus on the characteristics of the individual rather than on issues, politics reveals its candidate-centrism.

A large contributor to this feature of American politics is the incorporation of television into electoral campaigns. The simple fact of a medium designed to convey images creates an inherent bias toward appearance and visual engagement over other forms of connection and discourse. That facility in the medium has been exploited and advanced to a highly sophisticated level by journalistic practices. The orientation of many journalists toward scandal as a form of political entertainment combined with the nearly universal practice of covering campaigns as horse races rather than as debates over ideas and directions for the country have institutionalized candidate-centric politics. Candidates orient their strategies around the strengths of the medium, avoiding commitments to programs of action in favor of looking and sounding appealing as an individual.

Our analysis of the American public's reaction to campaign Web sites in 2000 suggests that the twentieth-century revolution in candidate-centrism has left unfulfilled a desire on the part of some citizens for information about issues. Citizens in our surveys who were highly engaged with the traditional mass media wanted to know more about national candidates' positions on issues than they were being told in newspapers and on television. As we saw in chapters 4 and 5, a major reason that supporters of national candidates visit their sites is to search out information about issues; for those making a return visit, issue information is even more important as a motivation. Learning about issues is also implicated in strengthening citizens' feelings toward their favored candidate. In the state-level races, issue information was even more important than in national races, which reinforces the conclusion that mass media leave a substantial level of citizen demand for issue information unsatisfied.

But the fact that citizens learned more about candidates as people than about their issue positions in the state races provides a kind of back-handed endorsement of at least some media attention to candidates as personalities. Voters want information about the people who are running for office as people, and this may be the first kind of information they learn about candidates who are less than highly familiar to them. In this sense, the practice of the mass media in pro-

158

viding news about campaigns for office as stories of contests between personalities does indeed satisfy a real demand by citizens. By all appearances it overwhelms that demand with far more coverage of personality than voters may want, but the media hardly misjudge altogether in their framing of politics in personal terms.

At a practical level, these findings suggest that highly visible candidates for office might increase the effectiveness of their Web sites at motivating supporters by focusing on issue information, especially the kind that compares candidates' positions. Since many supporters who visit Web sites are likely to be more issue oriented in the first place, for them, reinforcement requires substantive content beyond a candidate's superficial personal characteristics.

At a deeper level, we interpret this finding as a kind of natural experiment posed by the Internet. For several decades, news media have provided citizens a larger and larger diet of candidate-centric information and a smaller and smaller diet of issue information. Now, a new medium has arisen that permits citizens to choose what they want from a huge and varied menu: biographies of candidates, images, video, news, cheerleading about the candidate, and in most cases a substantial selection of information about issues. Citizens' actions in choosing from this menu can signal what they desire and what interests them in a way that their use of television and newspapers does not. The signal we observe is that mass media tell voters by and large all they want to know about their favorite candidates as individuals and not enough about candidates as advocates of issue positions. This is hardly the first sign of the importance of issues to voters, but we find it especially compelling. Even broadcast attack ads have been shown to improve voters' knowledge of candidates' positions on issues.[25]

The Internet's contribution toward political transparency is related. Particularly in the statement of issue positions, Web sites can commit candidates to document their positions on issues to a degree that other media do not. Candidates place issue statements on their Web sites; they do it early in the campaigns; and they typically provide a reasonably high level of specificity. Compared with the level of written, documented issue information released by campaigns via other channels, this specificity and transparency is in many cases quite remarkable. It would seem to complement voters' own taste for more concrete information about issues than the mass media typically provide. It is possible that this kind of transparency will lead candidates to hold more consistent positions, although other aspects of the technology permit campaigns to segment what different citizens see and how issues are emphasized.

From the perspective of the campaigns themselves, this transparency is not necessarily desirable. The laying out of these positions can alter the strategic game between campaigns and reduce some of the suspense of the race. As one staffer we interviewed noted: "From a policy research perspective, it makes it hard for there to be any surprises. We knew what they'd use . . . and they knew what we'd use. All the information is out there. Both sides know what everybody's got."

A second effect involves political learning. Users of candidate Web sites do learn from their exposure to candidate online information, and the greatest gain in information levels comes in the least publicized races. This clearly shows that Internet political information can be particularly valuable in races where the news media fail to offer substantive information about candidates—or even any information at all!

As the news media offer decreasing amounts of information about campaigns, the Internet may become the source for such information, particularly for those who hunger for greater substance. Yet, this online audience may not be those most in need of such information. Those who could be hurt most by the decline in traditional news media coverage may be the voters who are least likely to obtain substitute information online. These are citizens who receive political information passively via traditional media sources, but who are not inclined to be proactive in searching for such information.

The other group—those who are proactive in acquiring political information—make fewer gains from Internet exposure in terms of learning about candidates. Why is that? These voters do seek information online and learn from it, but they approach this process with strong preconceptions about the information they find. They search for issue information helpful in reinforcement. It may be surprising to some that voters gain this information *after* they have candidate preferences. But the problem is not the voters, but expectations of them. Voters, whether online or not, usually make candidate decisions based on their party affiliation, the influence of family and friends, and their own personal interests and values. That their long-standing approach to making vote choices is carried into their online activity should really come as no surprise.

Nevertheless, there are two major reasons why we are sanguine about this process. One is that the process of learning can fortify citizens' commitment and interest, and that strengthening lays the groundwork for engagement—for voting, for volunteering, for working in the public arena—even if it did not in 2000 produce measurable gains in actual engagement. Any factor with a potential to strengthen that foundation is desirable.

Another positive benefit is the level of citizen intellectual engagement with politics. We believe that the better citizens are able to develop informed rationales and arguments in favor of their political orientations, the higher the overall level of political dialogue. Democracy is clearly stronger the more deliberative it is, and one of the elementary requirements of deliberation is that citizens be able to offer others reasons for their political views and preferences. Our analysis certainly provides no evidence that campaign Web sites harm this aspect of deliberation and engagement on the part of partisans and engaged citizens. On the contrary, campaign sites show potential to improve these aspects. This potential is especially striking when viewed in explicit comparison with television.

This is not to suggest that the Internet will reverse the trend toward candidate-centrism nor inform the uninformed among Americans. Selectivity largely precludes the latter; on that, our evidence is unequivocal. As for the former, we emphasize how important television remains in national election campaigns. It is as strong as ever as it influences how politics is conducted, who wins and loses, and the ways that citizens think about democracy. We simply find that campaign Web sites work differently and have the potential to satisfy a demand for substantive information that is unmet by the still-dominant mode of communication.

We see evidence that through use of the Internet by campaigns, supporters of candidates can become more engaged even if the effect is not overwhelming in scale and even if it is primarily online. If at least some politically interested individuals can find a channel for their desire for activism, that would be an attractive development.

In historical perspective, two comparisons with previous "new" media are important. The first is with television. The trend of television's role in politics has been to mediate the linkages among voters and candidates and to contribute to the spectator-versus-activist role of citizens. This disconnecting process has been helped by a number of other trends, such as changes in the electoral system, increased incumbency protection, and the growing complexity of political issues. While television has distanced voters from parties and candidates, the Internet offers at least some opportunities for reconnection among the politically interested.

By contrast, mass newspapers—the "penny press"—emerged in the 1820s and 1830s, facilitated by the new technology of high-speed printing and the emergence of a new business model. This new form reduced the cost of a newspaper copy to one-sixth the going rate of earlier newspapers, which had been designed more for elites.[26] These newspapers were highly political and highly partisan. Throughout much of the nineteenth century, ties between papers and parties were strong, although they had weakened considerably by the dawn of the twentieth century. This era before the professionalization of journalism was not one, though, in which partisanship in news turned off voters. On the contrary, the highly political news, connected during election time with party rallies, torchlight processions, and brass bands, appears to have helped sustain citizens' engagement with politics.

Toward the end of the nineteenth century, Progressive Era reforms curtailed many party functions.[27] Similarly, journalism entered a new phase of "objectivity," which still is the dominant theme, even with the recent shift toward interpretive journalism. It brought about the end of the partisan press. The result was the modern professional newspaper, officially nonpartisan and dedicated to objectivity as a standard. While the function of objective information dissemination was furthered, other functions were weakened, including the reinforcement and mobilization of voters to participate in the electoral process.

Following the rise of the modern newspaper and the implementation of political changes weakening the party, voter turnout declined. The cleaning up of partisan and often corrupt political influence during the Progressive Era coincided with a decades-long slump in voting participation. Whatever else they felt about parties and progressivism in a democracy, Americans were far less interested in voting in 1920 than they had been in 1880 as a result of all these changes.[28] The decline of the party newspaper and its replacement with the modern paper is part of this story.

Although the comparison with television is the more common correlation used by Internet watchers, we suggest that the newspaper of the nineteenth century may be the more accurate analogy. In the very modest tendency of the Internet to provide new means of connection among engaged, committed citizens and candidates, we hear faint echoes not of television but of a once-partisan press.

The third effect we observed is perhaps the most intriguing of all, though least conclusive so far from a scientific perspective. It involves the differences in dynamics between well-known and lesser-known candidates. Our findings showed that the audiences for minor-party candidates are different from those of major-party candidates. These less well known candidates do tend to draw people who are more curious politically. And citizens appear to learn more from these sites—no doubt because of the relative paucity of information available in mass media.

Much has been made of the fact that the Web provides a means for resource-poor candidates to address the public. We find some support for this effect. The fact that roughly half as many people who saw the Gore Web site saw the Nader site is impressive compared with the imbalance in television coverage that plagues minor-party candidates. A minor-party candidate can benefit from even limited exposure in traditional media if curious voters then turn to the candidate's Web site for more information. Given the extensive use of traditional news media sources by online political site visitors, this scenario is quite plausible.

However, the problem of the limited reach of online candidate communication still minimizes such an effect. Visitors to candidate

Web sites tend to be those who are already politically interested rather than typical voters. Moreover, the 2000 election may be an aberration in the fact that swing voters remained indecisive until late in the campaign, thus enhancing the willingness of some online voters to explore alternatives.

It is true, as many say, that those citizens seeking information about alternatives to the Democrats and Republicans can now find it readily, even as traditional media continue their focus on the major candidates. On the other hand, selectivity effects remain very powerful. People strongly committed to a Republican or Democratic candidate do not often visit the Web site of a minor-party candidate. Citizens who have little awareness of minor-party candidates are hardly likely to seek out and visit their Web sites.

This means that campaign sites cannot provide the leverage that non–major-party candidates like Ralph Nader or Pat Buchanan need to gain office. Such candidates face heavy barriers—the lack of previous political experience, systems of representation and electoral rules designed to exclude them, the socialization of citizens to conceptualize American politics in terms of two-party competition, and, in most cases, extremist ideologies (or, at least, extreme issue positions)—that make their candidacies unpalatable to most voters. These are sufficient to limit the success of these candidates. But the media practices of emphasizing major candidates and of approaching elections as horse races rather than contests among ideas and policy positions support the marginalization of minor-party candidates stemming from legal and social foundations. These media practices are self-perpetuating. Journalists writing horse-race stories focus little attention on minor parties because those candidates have little chance of competing well and forming part of the exciting and dramatic aspect of the election. That lack of coverage then helps keep minor-party candidates uncompetitive and therefore unnewsworthy.

Our study shows that the Internet will not level the playing field for minor-party candidates, as some may have expected. It may, when coupled with at least some traditional media coverage, provide campaigns with a comparatively low-cost way to distribute the candidate's message to that currently small percentage of voters who are curious about other candidates beyond those from the two major parties.

The Internet and the Future of Elections

Our conclusion of a weak electoral effect of the Internet likely satisfies no one. Those who see the Internet as a solution to various electoral problems, such as the inability of minor parties to compete effectively or increasing citizen cynicism regarding elections, will be disappointed. From the other side of the spectrum, those who see the Internet as a worthless and unproven campaign gimmick also may not be happy with our results, since they suggest that the Internet can serve reinforcing functions. The glass is half full in the sense that we have found the Internet capable of performing some important functions in campaigns, particularly functions that traditional media increasingly are abandoning. These include reinforcing political attachments and mobilizing potential activists to donate, volunteer, and—just maybe—to vote. The Internet also provides an information source for voters who seek more data to bolster their vote choices.

These are hardly unimportant functions. Yet, they lack the drama of early predictions about what effects the Internet would have on American democracy, including the electoral process, and therefore they may seem minor in comparison with expectations. Nevertheless, this outcome offers a more realistic picture of the Internet's role in American elections. From this portrayal, we can offer some predictions about the Internet and future elections.

1. The Internet's supplemental role in American
electoral campaigns will solidify as a form of niche
communication directed at highly specific audiences.

Television advertising offers several important similarities to campaign Web sites. Both present an advocacy position rather than news, and both are constructed and delivered by the candidate without the involvement of intermediary news organizations. That is, television ads and Web sites both present exclusively candidate-controlled messages.

It is clear from survey research and laboratory experiments that political advertising has consequences for voters' political knowledge about candidates and issues and for voters' feelings toward candidates. A number of studies show that television advertisements are more influential on voters' perceptions and knowledge of candidates than are other sources, such as newspapers, debates, and personal conversations.[29] These influences are strongest early in campaign seasons, especially during primary races, and also tend to be stronger among voters who remain undecided long into the campaign.[30] Not surprisingly, multiple exposures to advertisements have a greater effect than a single exposure.[31] Also, and perhaps most important for comparison with the Internet, television advertising appears to offer little capacity to persuade Democrats to vote for Republicans or vice versa. Exposure to opposition advertisements may even strengthen the loyalty of voters to their favored candidate or party.[32] Hence, reinforcement becomes the most prevalent outcome.

Any expectation of the Internet as primarily an instrument for voter conversion is a vain one. But as a tool for reaching a select audience and achieving significant campaign functions, the Internet promises to have a bright future as a campaign tool.

2. The Internet will offer campaigns a new and highly effective tool for mobilizing activists.

This role is not limited to electoral campaigns but also may be significant in processes involving collective associations and interest group politics.[33] For candidates, however, it is a crucial activity, particularly as the traditional party organizational ties have weakened.

Candidates need media capable of identifying, reinforcing, and mobilizing activists. Such resources have been in short supply since the decline of party organizations and partisan media. The Internet will be an important tool for such campaign functions.

3. Citizens who are politically interested and active increasingly will utilize the Internet as a vehicle for satisfying their need for information and support.

Internet activity will not be a replacement for traditional campaign functions, particularly for less traditional media-oriented campaigns, such as state or local races. Rather, Internet activity will merge into traditional campaign activities. The 2000 campaign was an example of such integration as campaigns used e-mail, telephone calling, and personal contact to reach voters. Voters, even those online, will continue to want both online and traditional forms of contact with candidates, such as appearances at rallies or debates or even door-to-door contact. Voters know that e-mail is the easiest form of contact, but also a highly impersonal one.

4. The Internet will not produce the mobilization of voters long predicted.

The much-vaunted Internet election of 2000 coincided with a highly competitive presidential election, extensive Internet usage by campaigns, and Internet access finally reaching a majority of Americans. It would be hard to find better conditions for the Internet's role as the impetus for a change in the direction of voter turnout. Yet, voter turnout remained low.

The problem for the Internet is the necessity of having an active audience making a conscious choice to view political sites. That choice is much more intentional than with television or newspapers because the Internet user can choose from among literally millions of potential sites for viewing. As one campaign staffer noted, "The Web site is good at mobilizing people, but not at bringing people in. There has to be active interest for people to go to the site, and most of those people are people who have already decided."[34]

Even e-mail, which candidates can use to attempt to overcome the barrier of voters' passivity, has the limit of online social mores. Campaigns are reluctant to spam unsuspecting voters, from whom they expect to get more hostility than curiosity. One minor-party presidential campaign said that it was offered e-mail addresses from a political Web site, but declined to buy them. Yet, such usage may become more common in the future. This practice may mean risking the wrath of a group of voters, but it may be the only way to push the mobilization message out much as television advertising does during prime-time entertainment programs. Due to forces of selectivity producing political avoidance, the trends of declining voter involvement will not be stemmed by the existence of the Internet. If such trends are to be reversed, other means will have to be found. In fact, the Internet carries the potential to exacerbate the problem. Therefore,

5. The divide between those who
are political activists interested in electoral
campaigns and those who are not
will expand.

Traditional media may justify decreasing campaign coverage on the view that voters can turn to the Internet for issue information or even candidate backgrounds. Yet, most citizens will not seek out nor utilize online electoral information. Their levels of political knowledge may decline while those who do make use of online political sources will learn more about candidates and campaigns, particularly issue information.

So the Internet may not expand the electorate and cure the ailments of the electoral system. But it will breathe new life into parts of the electoral process as candidates adopt still another way to do what they must do to win—reach interested voters—and those voters, in turn, find new means to become engaged in this vital process of representative government.

In this study, we have addressed ourselves strictly to one area of democracy: electoral campaigns and voting behavior. This is hardly the sum total of democratic processes nor even the totality of political players and organizations. We have not evaluated directly the consequences of the Internet for many elements of politics: the ongoing role of the mass media between elections, the nature of political organizations and interest groups, processes of policy making, the health of civil society and political culture, and more. While it is beyond the scope of any one study to assess all of these topics, we do wish to take a step back from the specifics of election campaigns and consider briefly how what we have found reflects on the larger issue of the Internet in American democracy.

In the area of campaigning for office, the focus of our study, the requirements and dynamics of media coverage have become the organizing principle of democracy. It is not merely that candidates rooted in a system of political institutions and committed to issues and sets of constituencies must employ the media to run for office. That kind of system is a requirement of any democracy larger than a village. The problem is that candidates have become rooted in a system of media reliance, and they engage issues, political institutions, and constituencies from that media-centric position. As Thomas Patterson argues in his classic critique, *Out of Order*, we no longer simply employ the media in our democratic contests, we organize those contests around the media.[35]

What then of the Internet? Our analysis of campaigning using the Internet offers little reason to believe that any major changes in this trend are at hand. We see little in the dynamics of the Internet that would hint at the transcendence of politics beyond media-centrism. Candidates still need to rely on traditional media in order to reach the masses of voters who never will subscribe to a political e-mail list or visit a candidate Web site. For this vast majority of voters, the media-centric nature of campaigns has not been diminished.

Our study shows that the vast majority of Internet users are not utilizing this opportunity to bypass the traditional media because they are ignoring candidate sites altogether. Those relative few who are, though, find in online candidate communication the information that has been lacking in their traditional media diet.

Supplementing rather than displacing may be the pattern in other intersection points between the Internet and American political processes and institutions, as well as in individual citizen behavior. While maintaining allegiance to traditional media sources, select groups of citizens may turn to the Internet for supplemental sources of information, not only about elections, but also about public policy.

Traditional media are affected by this new medium. As discussed earlier, the traditional news outlets may see less urgency to fill the needs of a politically interested audience. Traditional broadcast news media served large, diverse audiences and attempted to satisfy the range of audience tastes. New outlets, such as cable and satellite news options, have lopped off the part of the audience interested in larger doses of political information. As a result, this audience is served less by traditional evening news programs, which feature increasing amounts of soft news for the less politically interested audience remaining. The Internet may add to that erosion, accelerating the movement away from political news.[36]

This said, we do not believe that the Internet will create the highly polarized, fragmented audiences that some fear, any more than it will create a large-scale virtual community. The Web does indeed facilitate selective thinking to a greater extent than other media, therefore leading toward more polarization and fragmentation. Journalist David Weinberger captures this idea by observing that while the mass media give everyone their Warholian 15 minutes of fame, the Internet permits everyone to be famous among 15 people.[37]

But this trend is likely to be far more limited in extent than some have worried. In his book *Republic.com*, for instance, legal scholar Cass Sunstein visits technologist Nicholas Negroponte's idea of the "daily me," a society of individuals each receiving their own customized, tailored, personalized version of news and communication. Sunstein is rightly aghast at the political consequences of such a vision. He asks us to "[s]uppose, for example, that people with a certain political conviction find themselves learning about more and more authors with the same view, and thus strengthening their existing judgments, only because most of what they are encouraged to read says the same thing. In a democratic society, might this not be troubling?"[38] Our study certainly provides evidence for such selectivity, and we agree that in principle the result could be troubling if carried far enough.

We find, however, that Negroponte has it wrong factually, whatever one thinks of his normative vision. What is wrong is not his understanding of technology but his understanding of human behavior. The technologies of the Internet do indeed make the "daily me" a technological possibility. We see evidence that some people in some circumstances do indeed exploit this possibility. But the interdependence of traditional and new media suggests that few political Internet site users limit their received information to online sources.

170 The Internet does facilitate highly selective forms of engagement, but its effects are dependent upon broadcast media and traditional journalism. This interdependence suggests traditional media and new media are integrated by the citizen in his or her regular information-gathering routines, rather than the former being displaced by the latter.

The fact that the Internet supplements and augments the mass media rather than replacing them mitigates the tendency for fragmentation. The story of the Internet and democracy is not simply one of new media displacing old media, or old media maneuvering to capture the new. The Internet does not automatically support tendencies toward either centralization or decentralization. Rather, it maintains the inherent tension between these competing forces.

Appendix

Origins and General Design of the Project

Over dinner one evening at a Philadelphia restaurant, following a day-long Internet conference at the University of Pennsylvania, we shared with each other our individual plans for future research. Each of us had been studying and writing about new media in politics for several years. We found that we were both interested in studying the role of the Internet during the 2000 campaign. One of us had plans to content analyze candidate Web sites to examine how candidates presented themselves to voters. The other wanted to survey voters to determine how they react to candidate messages online. Hearing the other's plans, we each realized that our own work would provide just half of the picture of the Internet in elections. We decided to join forces. Our aim would be a fuller picture: how candidates use Web sites and how voters react to them.

Both of us had been frustrated at the paucity of systematic, detailed evidence about Americans' online behavior. Especially in the early years of the Internet, scientific data about voter use of Web sites were largely unavailable. The best available clues came from logs of "hits" on Web sites and from data gleaned from tracking identifiers—so-called cookies—placed by Web site sponsors on the computers of people who visited their sites. The fact that hit logs simply measure the number of times a page is seen does not tell us much about how individual voters actually use a Web site. They do not necessarily even tell us whether one person visited a Web site ten times or ten people visited once. Tracking identifiers, originally called "cookies," are not much better. Aside from the ethical question of whether people ought to have their activities tracked without their consent, these techniques also fail to reveal much of importance about the individuals behind the computers—their party identification, whether they had made up their minds whom to vote for before visiting the Web site, or virtually any other identifying information of social scientific relevance. To make matters worse, such systems cannot recognize the same person using two computers—perhaps one at work and one at home—nor differentiate among several people using the same computer, such as a family at home or dozens of people at a library.

Randomized surveys permit researchers to evaluate in great detail those individuals who agree to answer questions. For instance, we know from the American National Election Studies, a series of scientifically constructed academic surveys, that in 1996, about 6 percent of adults in the United States obtained information about the campaigns at least once through the Internet. This figure represented about a quarter of all people who had access to the Internet that year. We know also that by the 1998 elections, about 9 percent of adults reported obtaining campaign information through the Internet—a figure representing only a fifth of Internet users. By 2000, the figures had changed dramatically. Almost half of the people with Internet access (45 percent), which represents 24 percent of all U.S. adults, saw election information on the Internet.

The main limitation of surveys such as these is that they almost invariably are based on generalized random samples of about 1,000 to 2,000 Americans. This means that no more than a few hundred individuals in the survey used the Internet for any political purpose at all, and at most a couple of dozen people in the survey may have seen any particular Web site of interest. Such numbers are far too small to form the basis for useful statistical inferences about George Bush's web audience or about women who visited Al Gore's site. When general randomized surveys are used, the same problem plagues the study of other important groups whose numbers are not large in comparison to the whole population. For instance, general surveys of Americans typically pick up only a handful of African Americans, because they constitute only about 12 percent of the population. The result in such cases is that researchers are able to make far less thorough and solid inferences about African Americans as a subgroup than about the white population.

The way to overcome this problem scientifically is straightforward, but it is expensive and time consuming, so it is undertaken infrequently for the study of racial and other subgroups and had never been done for the study of Internet campaigns. Thus, we agreed in Philadelphia, we would collect random samples composed entirely of viewers of the Web sites of interest.

Given our prior interests and methodological approaches, it was clear our joint project would employ a multimethod technique. We would approach our research with a design capable of capturing the 2000 campaigns from several perspectives. We would evaluate the relationships among candidates and voters by examining the candidates' online messages, by talking to campaign officials, and by surveying the people who actually visited the candidates' Web sites. In our surveys, we knew we would need a special sample that was exclusively visitors to campaign Web sites and a control sample of people who did not see a site, in order to make comparisons. We also wanted to supplement the survey with a laboratory experiment in which we could control very carefully what citizens saw and in which we could be more confident that problems of recall were not introducing error into our analysis. We ended up with a plan for a four-method study: content analyses of candidate Web sites, interviews with Webmasters and other campaign staff responsible for the strategy of the online campaign effort, random-digit dialing surveys, and a Web-based experiment. (Later we describe further the details of our experimental and survey techniques and discuss their respective merits.)

We chose presidential candidates because they represent the common experience for voters across the nation. Every voter interacts with the presidential candidates at least through the decision-making process that results in a vote choice. Studying the major-party candidates of the Democrats and the Republicans was obvious, but we also decided to include minor-party candidates. The 2000 campaign was unusual in this regard since it featured two well-known minor-party candidates: Ralph Nader (Green party) and Patrick Buchanan (Reform party). The Reform party had received over 8 percent of the popular vote in the last election, while the Green candidate was polling above 5 percent in some national surveys in the fall. While it was clear this was not a competitive four-way race by any means, it was certainly not a typical two-party contest: Both Buchanan and Nader had the potential to be a factor in the outcome. In our interviews and content analyses, we also included John Hagelin, who fought a late battle with Buchanan over the Reform party nomination. We did not, however, include Hagelin, who eventually ran on the Natural Law ticket, in our surveys or experiment.

In addition to looking at the presidential races, we also wanted to examine statewide races. State races figured prominently in our research plans from the beginning because they can differ in so many ways from presidential contests. State races typically receive less attention in the mass media than presidential races, and in some cases the candidates themselves are less well known. Our theory told us that the dynamics of Internet-based campaigns should be highly dependent upon the dynamics of mass media coverage, and so we viewed state-level races as an excellent way to explore the relationship between new and old media. Examining some state-level Web sites and interviewing campaign staff would be a straightforward extension of our national research design. Surveying states would present a greater challenge. It is not useful statistically simply to break apart a national survey of typical size and scale to look at states individually. Scientific sampling techniques require essentially a new survey in every state one wishes to study. This meant that to look at state races we would have to replicate our national survey at the state level.

Our approach was to choose one state that would be as typical as we could find on the relevant characteristics and to focus our efforts there. We began with a list of criteria and worked through them, eliminating states until we had a unique choice. First, we wanted a state with competitive Senate and governor's races in 2000, which would mean active Web efforts on the part of all four major-party candidates and would also mean that the outcome of both would be decided in the campaigning rather than before the races even began. This would permit us to examine two races with one survey. Second, we wanted a state of at least moderate electoral significance, and we drew the line at about eight or nine electoral college votes. Third, we wanted a state that was typical in patterns of computer ownership or Internet use.

Only one state met these criteria: Missouri. The Senate race there was particularly compelling. Governor Mel Carnahan was running for Senate against the incumbent, Senator John Ashcroft. For governor, Representative Jim Talent was running against State Treasurer Bob Holden. Both of these races would be strongly contested. As for electoral impact, Missouri's 11 electoral college votes make it of moderate importance. (Had Missouri gone the other way in 2000, Al Gore would have been elected president.) In addition, Missouri has the attractive feature of being a bellwether state in American politics. Over the past quarter century, Missourians have delivered their electoral votes to such diverse candidates as Jimmy Carter, Ronald Reagan, George H. W. Bush, and Bill Clinton. Interestingly, the state has voted with the winning presidential candidate every election over the past quarter century. As a border state, Missouri bridges the South and Midwest, and it is demographically standard with large urban areas (St. Louis and Kansas City), suburbs, and rural communities.

The tragic development during the campaign prompted us to modify our Missouri plans somewhat. The death of Governor Mel Carnahan on October 16, 2000, in a plane crash interrupted the Senate campaign. Senator Ashcroft ceased campaigning for a few days, and then eventually returned to the campaign trail, only to lose the race eventually to Carnahan, whose death came too late under Missouri law for a new candidate to be named. We had already archived versions of the Carnahan and Ashcroft sites up to that point, but since the Carnahan site became a memorial site following the candidate's death, we did not include further archiving of these candidates' sites. We made a last-minute change to our survey wording in Missouri to remove direct questions about the recently deceased and popular governor, as a matter of sensitivity and courtesy. Instead of asking direct questions about Carnahan, we asked more general questions of Missourians about the Senate race. Also, in our laboratory experiment in St. Louis (discussed later), we substituted for the Web sites of Carnahan and Ashcroft the sites of the candidates for secretary of state, Matt Blunt and Steve Gaw.

Our national-level Web audience survey also included questions about voter reaction to three nonpartisan voter information sites: Project Vote Smart, Freedom Channel, and DemocracyNet. We were interested to see who were the audiences of these sites and how they might differ from the audiences for candidates' own Web sites. For the most part, we found that the audience profiles were similar. None of the key findings we developed from looking at the candidate sites were altered by consideration of the nonpartisan sites. Therefore, in the analysis throughout the book, we largely omit discussion of these sites.

Detailed Description of Research Methods

Web Site Content Analysis

Content analysis is one of the best known and most widely utilized methods of studying mass communication.[1] Content analysis has certain advantages: unobtrusiveness in the communication interaction, replication, and relative low cost for gathering data.[2] Content analysis is a way of making inferences about people by examining what they say—in this case, what they say through the Internet. Since we wanted to make inferences about what messages candidates seek to tell voters, we looked at the content of their Web sites.

178   In this study, our unit of analysis was the candidate Web site. The presidential campaign sites (Bush, Gore, Nader, Buchanan, and Hagelin) and the state-level sites in Missouri were coded for components of the candidate's self-presentation. Because candidate sites typically change during the course of the campaign (particularly in high-profile campaigns), each site was downloaded twice during the course of the fall campaign for subsequent coding. These downloads occurred in mid-October and the day before the general election.

We also charted changes in the sites over that period of time. Although the number of items in some sections changed (such as news releases or texts of speeches), there was little change in the sites between the two dates. This finding confirmed that the sites remained largely intact during the period of our study: mid-October until early November.

Site coding entailed downloading the sites and archiving them using HTTrack, which is a browser utility that allows the user to download a Web site and view it offline. While the text was intact following this download, not all images and graphics were obtained for all sites. However, since our main objective was the textual content, that was not an obstacle. We coded the sites using an exhaustive coding instrument. This instrument examined not only the existence but also the placement of various aspects of candidates' Web presentations. Research assistants coded for the presence and placement of—as well as salience accorded—facets such as the candidate's personal presentation, issue substance, group/media endorsements, graphic design, negative campaigning, interactivity with users, facilitation of online action by users, identification of volunteers, solicitation of financial contributions, links to other sites, and so on.

Each presidential candidate site was coded by three coders. The composite reliability score for the three coders was 0.81. This counted as "agreement" only when there was unanimity across all three coders. When "agreement" was defined as two-thirds agreement, the score rose to 0.96.[3] There was unanimity among the coders on 59 percent of the 835 variables (167 variables for each candidate). On another 30 percent of the variables, there was two-thirds agreement among the coders. Pair-wise comparison of the coders found that agreement ranged from a low of 76 percent between coders 2 and 3 and a high of 82 percent between coders 1 and 2.

The level of agreement obviously differed depending on the nature of the variable. Most (75) variables were dichotomous, and coders merely noted the presence or absence of the variable. These included variables such as whether there was a Spanish version of the site, whether an issues section existed, and whether there was mention of the opponent. Intercoder reliability was 0.89 on those variables.

Ninety-two variables were nondichotomous. These included variables such as the listing of specific issues on the site or the number and type of photographs throughout the site. Intercoder reliability was not as high for these more complex variables: 0.71.

A similar process was used for nonpresidential candidate sites. There were six Missouri statewide candidate sites coded (two for governor, two for U.S. senator, and two for secretary of state). The composite reliability score for the three coders for these sites was 0.85. This counted as agreement only when there was unanimity across all three coders. When agreement was defined as two-thirds agreement, the score rose to 0.97. We obtained unanimity among the coders on 65 percent of the 1,128 variables (188 variables for each candidate). On another 26 percent of the variables, there was two-thirds agreement among the coders.

As with the presidential sites, the level of agreement obviously differed depending on the nature of the variable. Most variables (88) were dichotomous, and coders merely noted the presence or absence of the variable. These included variables such as whether there was a Spanish version of the site, whether an issues section existed, or whether there was mention of the opponent. Intercoder reliability was 0.90 on those variables. One hundred variables were nondichotomous. These included variables such as the listing of specific issues on the site or the number and type of photographs throughout the site. Intercoder reliability was not as high for these more complex variables: 0.79.

Interviews

The Web sites provided the public result of decisions made by campaigns regarding Internet use. We wanted to determine what those decisions were and why they were made. As one communications scholar has noted, "The Internet does not exist in isolation."[4] The decisions made regarding the Internet fit within a larger strategy of campaigning. We wanted to know how that fit occurred. The best ones to tell us were the creators of the Web sites and other campaign staffers who understood the role of the Web and e-mail in fulfilling the objectives of the campaign.

Appendix

Therefore, we conducted telephone or in-person interviews during and soon after the November elections. We or our research assistants conducted interviews with the campaign Webmasters for the major presidential campaigns—Bush, Gore, Nader, and Buchanan—and for the Missouri races, including gubernatorial candidates Jim Talent and Bob Holden, Senate candidate John Ashcroft, and the candidates for secretary of state, Matt Blunt and Steve Gaw. In addition to the Webmasters, we also interviewed other campaign officials, including campaign managers, communications directors, and press secretaries, who had some responsibility for the coordination of Internet strategy in their respective campaigns.

To provide perspective for the use of the Internet in the 2000 general election campaign, we also interviewed others who had been involved in Internet usage by candidates during the 2000 primaries and the 1998 elections. These included personnel involved with the presidential campaigns of Bill Bradley and John McCain, as well as Senator McCain himself.

National Surveys

Our survey techniques all involved random-digit dial sampling. When we were planning for our surveys, we used past American National Election Studies data to produce a working estimate that at least 5 percent of adults would visit at least one of the presidential sites we were studying during the 2000 general election campaign. We budgeted and scheduled our national Web audience survey using that figure and a goal of 1,000 respondents, which turned out to be quite safe and conservative.

Our survey instrument was designed to answer a wide variety of questions about respondents' use of the Internet and other media for campaign information and vote choice. The question batteries addressed the following:

1. demographics, including race, age, gender, occupation, annual household income, and marital status
2. political identification and interest, such as party identification and level of interest in the campaign

3. vote choice, such as awareness of candidates and intended vote
4. exposure to traditional media campaign coverage, including television news, magazines, newspapers, and paid political advertisements
5. general Internet use, including amount of use, length of time online, and usage of political information
6. e-mail use, such as amount and volume of personal e-mail as well as political e-mail
7. exposure to candidate web sites, including which sites were visited and how often
8. response to campaign sites, including motivations for the visit, self-rating of knowledge about the candidate before visiting, candidate preference before visiting the site, overall rating of the usefulness of the site, knowledge of about a half dozen aspects of the site (such as issue content, use of negative campaigning, graphic presentation), rating of the effect of the site on decision whether to vote, rating of the effect of the site on decision whether to donate money or volunteer, rating of the effect of the site on vote choice, and comparison of the value of the site to other sources of information

Our measure of knowledge was adapted from the test known as the Delli Carpini and Keeter Five. The questions were: (1) What job or political office is now held by Al Gore? (2) What job or political office is now held by William Rehnquist? (3) Whose responsibility is it to determine if a law is constitutional or not? Is it the president, Congress, or the Supreme Court? (4) How much of a majority is required for the U.S. Senate and House to override a presidential veto? (5) Do you happen to know which party had the most members in the House of Representatives in Washington before the election this/next month? (6) Would you say that one of the parties is more conservative than the other at the national level? If so, which one?

Research shows that responses to these questions accurately predict performance on much longer and more extensive tests of political knowledge. We compared scores on this test across people who had seen the various Web sites. We assumed that this battery of questions measured voters' baseline knowledge about politics independent of any effects from the Web sites they had seen.

To measure the reasons that people visited campaign sites, we asked people in our surveys an open-ended question about why they had first visited any of the Web sites they had seen. This question permitted the respondents to provide any answer that came to mind. Their responses varied quite widely, encompassing motivations such as learning about the candidate as an individual, obtaining news about the campaigns, learning about the candidate's positions on issues, and even obtaining campaign material or paraphernalia. In order to organize these thousand or so responses, we developed categories for classifying them. Our procedure was to create categories for each unique response, adding new categories until the smallest two contained 2 percent or less of the responses. This technique produced nine broad categories of reasons that people visit candidate Web sites.

The flow of the survey questions was flexible and responded to how many campaign sites each interviewee had seen. The mean time our survey staff spent with each respondent was 15 minutes, with the longest reaching 47 minutes. The survey was conducted by Wirthlin Worldwide, a commercial survey research firm specializing in political polling. The survey was in the field October 12–November 4. Wirthlin staff dialed phone numbers 142,552 times, with an average number of attempts per telephone number of 4. We reached 14,816 households where an adult spoke to the interviewer. Of those, 1,399 had Internet access and reported having seen at least one of the sites. Of those, 379 interviews stopped before reaching the last question, and we dropped all of these from the sample. This left us with a total of 1,020 respondents. The incidence rate for having seen at least one of the national Web sites (Bush, Gore, Nader, Buchanan, Freedom Channel, Project Vote Smart, or DemocracyNet) was 9.44 percent.

We also drew a random comparison sample from our 14,816 households, which consisted of 1,000 people who had not seen a presidential Web site, either because they did not have Internet access or because they simply never chose to visit. This sample provided us with a source of statistical comparison throughout our research.

We also conducted two follow-up surveys known as panel-back studies. One was conducted on November 8–9 and included 301 respondents from the national survey. Follow-up questions included vote turnout and vote choice, as well as what sources (including Web sites) influenced the vote decision. The second was conducted three months following the election and included a different 339 participants from the original 1,000. Questions asked in this survey included attention to the Florida election story, the actions of the new administration, and activities of the new Congress. Figure A.1 shows schematically the construction of these four national samples.

State Survey

Our statewide survey in Missouri used the same general random-digit telephone approach, but lacked the comparison and panel-back surveys. We made calls between October 20 and November 6. Callers dialed 59,256 numbers with the average number of attempts per telephone number again at 4. In total, 6,567 Missouri households were contacted where an adult spoke with the interviewer. Of those, 686 had Internet access and had seen at least one of the Web sites, but 186 interviews were stopped before completion and were not included, leaving a total sample size of 500. For the Missouri study, the incidence rate of having seen a site was slightly higher than the national survey at 10.45 percent, which is to be expected because we included four statewide races in addition to the seven national sites. We used the same questionnaire, with additions for the state-level races.

Laboratory Experiment

We employed a laboratory experiment to complement our surveys for several reasons. Studying campaign effects with cross-sectional survey designs has a number of limitations. Recall effects are among the most important of these, especially in studies of broadcast political communications. In surveys, nontrivial numbers of survey respondents can fail to recall correctly whether they have seen political news or advertising. Stephen Ansolabehere and Shanto Iyengar found that among experimental subjects in a television advertising

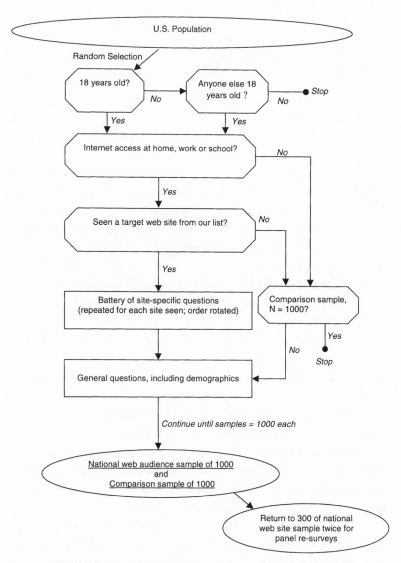

Figure A.1. Construction of the national Web audience sample, the national comparison sample, and the two panel-back samples

study, 20 percent of those shown no campaign advertisements recall having seen one in the study, while 50 percent of those shown an advertisement fail to remember having seen one a half hour later. As they argue, the fact that recall errors are likely to be correlated with variables of interest, such as political interest and knowledge, exacerbates the problem.[5]

On the other hand, the advantages of experimental research, such as avoiding reliance upon recall to establish whether a participant has been exposed to the stimulus in question, come at the cost of external validity. Exposing even the most carefully crafted groups of subjects to political communications under laboratory conditions can only approximate how citizens experience news and political information in vivo. One potentially important recall effect of a different kind may cause overestimation of campaign effects from experimental studies. Experimenters typically conduct postexperiment measurements of changed knowledge or attitudes immediately upon conclusion of the experimental condition. Such measurements tap short-term recall and impressions that may or may not prove lasting outside of the laboratory across days, weeks, or even months. Typically, what matters is how political communication affects citizens over time, for instance, on election day or when a political organization calls to ask for a donation or for action by citizens. Viewed in that light, the inaccurate recall that survey researchers encounter is not itself a problem but a part of the phenomenon of interest; experimental designs that proclaim communication effects to exist in general because they are detectable only minutes following exposure may in fact be more problematic.

Recall effects are likely to be less serious in surveys inquiring about political material on the Internet, because viewing political Web sites is an intentional act and therefore requires greater attention and cognition. Unlike broadcast advertising on television, which people view essentially by surprise while watching other content, campaign Web sites are only viewed by people who have made a decision to examine them. That intentionality proves vitally important to the politics and effects of campaign Web sites, and it also is likely to leave a stronger impression more readily and accurately accessible by survey methods than television advertising. For this reason, we believe survey research has a stronger capacity to detect correctly campaign effects in the case of Web sites than in the case of television advertising.

We ran our experiment in four cities in order to include the broadest possible cross section of citizens. We chose one city to represent each of the major regions of the country: New York City for the Northeast; Charlotte, North Carolina, for the Southeast; St. Louis for the Midwest and also to match our state-level analysis in Missouri; and San Diego, California, for the West. In each of these four cities, we used random-digit dialing techniques to call a random sample of people and invite them to a laboratory facility (either a hotel meeting room or a business office). Our goal was to assemble a group of laboratory subjects who would be the kind of people likely to visit a campaign site in the real world. We screened our invitees so that all had access to the Internet and reported using it at least once a week, and also all were registered voters. We aimed for a total of 50 participants in each city. Because the first 50 people who actually agree to participate in such a study are not random, even though our phone invitations started with a random sample, we used quota-based techniques to help maintain representativeness. From among those who agreed, we selected so that the resulting group of 50 in each city included a roughly equal balance by gender, education, and partisanship. Our requirements were that no group have more than 55 percent of one gender, that 35 percent $+/-$ 10 percent have a college degree, and that partisanship be within 5 percent of the following ratio: Republican, 40 percent; Democrat, 40 percent; and independent, 20 percent. Our incentive for participation was $50. The dates of our experiment were: San Diego (N=45), October 16–18; New York City (N=45), October 19–23; St. Louis (N=75), October 24–27; and Charlotte (N=45), October 30–November 1.

Researchers across many disciplines have found that it is literally impossible to assemble a truly random sample of Americans for laboratory experiments in the social sciences. Most researchers settle for residents of the single city where the researchers work, often without the use of quotas or randomization techniques. Worse yet, many studies rely on samples of undergraduate students. We believe that our four-city sample using random invitations and quota balancing improved upon previous media and politics experiments.

In the experiments, each respondent was given the opportunity to visit either the four presidential candidate sites, the three voter information sites, or, in St. Louis, the sites for the gubernatorial and secretary of state races. Respondents were placed in front of a computer either attached to a proxy server (N=105), which we operated with copies of the Web sites, or directly to the Internet and the candidates' live Web sites (N=105). Each respondent was given a packet of questions and a slip of paper, which contained four Web site names numbered 1 through 4. The respondent was instructed to fill out a pretest and then to go to the first Web site listed on the slip of paper. The respondents spent a few moments at that site at their discretion and then turned to their packet, where they were asked questions about the site they had just seen. They were then instructed to move on to another site and another set of questions until they were finished. This technique meant that by the second and third sites, the subjects knew what kinds of questions we were asking and were likely guided in their browsing to some extent by their anticipation of upcoming questions. We randomized the order in which subjects saw the sites, in order to prevent the data we collected about any particular site to be affected by its placement in the lineup. We accepted that each subject eventually developed a modicum of skill at critiquing Web sites, and we viewed that as useful in our research.

Note on Statistics

In order to avoid burdening readers who have a general interest in new media or politics but who lack research training or expertise in statistics, we have attempted to minimize the presentation of statistical details in this book. We have, however, employed bivariate and multivariate statistical analyses throughout our project. Our policy has been generally to report and describe differences between numbers (for example, 38 percent of the audience for presidential Web sites are women compared with 52 percent of people not among that audience) only when the differences are statistically significant at the 0.05 level or better, which means that the difference is not just the product of chance. A general rule of thumb is that any difference in percentages in our national surveys is meaningful statistically if equal to or greater than 3 percent, although this differs from one variable to another. Throughout the book, we have used notes to indicate statistical significance where it is not obvious from the discussion or from the figures themselves. In cases where we discuss the contribution of multiple factors to some outcome, we use OLS and logistic regressions to arrive at our conclusions. For instance, in chapter 4, the analysis of political knowledge uses an OLS model with variables for education, gender, age, partisanship, ideology, voting intention, interest, and income. The model R^2 is 0.27, and the significant variables are education, gender, age, and interest. More information on statistical models is available from the authors.

Notes

Chapter 1

1. Quoted in Barbara J. Saffir, "Weaving Their Webs: The Candidates Race to Cyberspace," *Washington Post*, July 23, 1995, p. C3.

2. For 1996 figures, see Dave D'Alessio, "Use of the World Wide Web in the 1996 U.S. Election, *Electoral Studies* 16 (1997): 489–500. For 2000 figures, see "Who's Online," at http://netelection.org. Major-party congressional candidates with Web sites are listed on www.freedomchannel.com as a ratio of total major-party congressional candidates. Freedom Channel listed 1,140 U.S. House candidates with Web sites, 805 of whom were major-party candidates.

3. Nielsen/NetRatings, at http://209.249.142.22/press_releases/pr_000817 .htm.

4. The Democracy Online Project, "Post-Election 2000 Survey on Internet Use for Civics and Politics," December 4, 2000, at http://democracyonline. org/databank/dec2000survey.shtml. Also see "Internet Election News Audience Seeks Convenience, Familiar Names," Pew Research Center for the People and the Press, December 3, 2000, at http://www.people-press.org/ online00rpt.htm. The authors' own survey shows that 28 percent of adults used the Internet in 2000 for one of five political purposes; see Bruce Bimber, *Information and American Democracy: Technology in the Evolution of Political Power* (Cambridge: Cambridge University Press, 2003).

5. Alexa Research, "Web Traffic Becoming Less Concentrated," press release, March 5, 2001, at http://www.alexaresearch.com/clientdir/news.

6. Supreme Court of the United States, Janet Reno, Attorney General of the United States v. et al., *Appellants v. American Civil Liberties Union et al.*, No. 96–511, June 26, 1997.

7. Dick Morris, *Vote.com* (New York: Renaissance, 1999); and Cass Sunstein, *Republic.com* (Princeton, N.J.: Princeton University Press, 2001).

8. For previous works addressing this question, see Anthony Corrado and Charles M. Firestone, eds., *Elections in Cyberspace: Toward a New Era in American Politics* (Washington, D.C.: Aspen Institute, 1996); Wayne Rash, Jr., *Politics on the Nets* (New York: W. H. Freeman, 1997); Gary W. Selnow, *Electronic Whistle-Stops: The Impact of the Internet on American Politics* (Westport, Conn.: Praeger, 1998); Richard Davis and Diana Owen, *New Media and American Politics* (New York: Oxford University Press, 1998); and Richard Davis, *The Web of Politics: The Internet's Impact on the American Political System* (New York: Oxford University Press, 1999).

9. One notable exception was Alexis de Tocqueville, who commented on the American newspaper as a feature of public life in his classic: *Democracy in America* (New York: Vintage Books [1840] 1945).

10. Exceptions include Angus Campbell, Gerald Gurin, and Warren E. Miller, "Television and the Election," *Scientific American* 188 (May 1953): 46–48; and Herbert A. Simon and Frederick Stern, "The Effect of Television upon Voting Behavior in Iowa in the 1952 Presidential Election," *American Political Science Review* 49 (June 1955): 470–77.

11. U.S. Department of Commerce, *Statistical Abstract of the United States, 1961* (Washington, D.C.: Government Printing Office, 1961), 516.

Chapter 2

1. Quoted in Robert J. Dinkin, *Campaigning in America: A History of Election Practices* (New York: Greenwood, 1989), 37.

2. Michael Schudson, *The Good Citizen* (Cambridge, Mass.: Harvard University Press, 1998).

3. For a discussion of the changes in the role of political party organizations, see David Broder, *The Party's Over* (New York: Harper and Row, 1972); Xandra Kayden and Eddie Mahe, Jr., *The Party Goes On* (New York: Basic, 1985); Larry J. Sabato, *The Party's Just Begun* (Glenview, Ill.: Scott Foresman/ Little, Brown, 1988); Alan Ware, *The Breakdown of Democratic Party Organization, 1940–1980* (New York: Oxford University Press, 1985); and A. James Reichley, *The Life of the Political Parties* (New York: Free Press, 1992).

4. See David Menefee-Libey, *The Triumph of Campaign-Centered Politics* (New York: Chatham, 2000); Martin P. Wattenberg, *The Decline of American Political Parties 1952–1996* (Cambridge, Mass.: Harvard University Press, 1998); and Martin P. Wattenberg, *The Rise of Candidate-Centered Politics:*

Presidential Elections in the 1980s (Cambridge, Mass.: Harvard University Press, 1991).

5. Herbert E. Alexander and Anthony Corrado, *Financing the 1992 Election* (Armonk, N.Y.: Sharpe, 1995), 235–37.

6. Brennan Center for Justice, "2000 Presidential Race First in Modern History Where Political Parties Spend More on TV Ads Than Candidates," press release, December 11, 2000, at http://www.brennancenter.org/press center/pressrelease_2000_1211cmag.html.

7. Michael J. Robinson, "Where's the Beef? Media and Media Elites in 1984," in *The American Elections of 1984*, ed. Austin Ranney (Durham, N.C.: Duke University Press/AEI, 1985), 172–77.

8. Quoted in F. Christopher Arterton, "Campaign Organizations Confront the Media Environment," in *Race for the Presidency*, ed. James David Barber (Englewood Cliffs, N.J.: Prentice Hall, 1978), 5.

9. Judith S. Trent and Robert V. Friedenberg, *Political Campaign Communication*, 2d ed. (New York: Praeger, 1991), 13; and Edie N. Goldenberg and Michael W. Traugott, *Campaigning for Congress* (Washington, D.C.: CQ Press, 1984), 112.

10. Center for Media and Public Affairs, "Campaign '96 Final: How TV News Covered the General Election," *Media Monitor*, November–December 1996, p. 1; and Paul Taylor, "Political Coverage in the 1990s: Teaching the Old News New Tricks," in *The New News v. The Old News: The Press and Politics in the 1990s* (Washington, D.C.: Twentieth Century Fund, 1992), 40–41.

11. Thomas E. Patterson, *Out of Order* (New York: Knopf, 1994), 73–75.

12. Catherine A. Steele and Kevin G. Barnhurst, "The Journalism of Opinion: Network News Coverage of U.S. Presidential Campaigns, 1968–1988," *Critical Studies in Mass Communication* 13 (September 1996): 187.

13. A meta-analysis of media bias in presidential elections confirmed a slight pro-Democratic bias in television network news campaign coverage. See Dave D'Alessio and Mike Allen, "Media Bias in Presidential Elections: A Meta-Analysis," *Journal of Communication* 50 (Autumn 2000): 133–56.

14. For a discussion of these trends, see Doug Underwood, *When MBAs Rule the Newsroom* (New York: Columbia University Press, 1993); and Alison Carper, "Marketing News," in *Politics and the Press*, ed. Pippa Norris (Boulder, Colo.: Lynne Rienner, 1997), 45–65.

15. For a discussion of the decline in congressional news coverage, see Timothy E. Cook, *Making Laws and Making News: Media Strategies in the U.S. House of Representatives* (Washington, D.C.: Brookings Institution, 1989); Robyn S. Goodman, "How Two Papers Covered President and Congress in China Trade Controversy," *Newspaper Research Journal* 19 (Fall 1998): 40; and Martin Weinberger, "Coverage: The Void at Home," *Media Studies Journal* 10 (Winter 1996): 101–7. For a discussion of the decline in

state government coverage, see Charles Layton and Mary Walton, "Missing the Story at the Statehouse," *American Journalism Review* (July–August 1998): 42.

16. See "Campaign 2000 Final: How TV News Covered the General Election Campaign," *Media Monitor*, November–December 2000, p. 2.

17. Center for the Media and Public Affairs, *Media Monitor*, January–February 2001, pp. 1–2.

18. Ibid.

19. Gallup Organization, "Confidence in Institutions," at http://www.gallup.com/poll/indicators/indconfidence.asp.

20. Andrew Kohut, "Public Support for the Watchdogs Is Fading," *Columbia Journalism Review* (May–June 2001): 52; and "Big Doubts about the News Media's Values," Pew Research Center for the People and the Press, February 25, 1999, at http://www.people-press.org/feb99rpt.htm.

21. For an extensive discussion of the new media's role in American politics, see Richard Davis and Diana Owen, *New Media and American Politics* (New York: Oxford University Press, 1998).

22. Ibid., 7.

23. Thomas L. Friedman, "The Inauguration: Clinton Takes Oath as 42d President, Urging Sacrifice to 'Renew America,'" *New York Times*, January 21, 1993, p. A1.

24. Todd S. Purdum, "A Kiss for the Ages," *New York Times*, September 24, 2000, sec. 4, p. 2.

25. Caryn James, "Bush Flunks Letterman's Late-Night Examination," *New York Times*, March 2, 2000, p. A22.

26. Pippa Norris, *A Virtuous Circle: Political Communications in Postindustrial Societies* (New York: Cambridge University Press, 2001), 137–61.

27. See, for example, Anthony Corrado and Charles M. Firestone, eds., *Elections in Cyberspace: Toward a New Era in American Politics* (Washington, D.C.: Aspen Institute, 1996); Phil Noble, "Net the Vote," *Campaigns & Elections*, July 1996, p. 27; and Barbara J. Saffir, "Weaving Their Webs: The Candidates Race to Cyberspace," *Washington Post*, July 23, 1995, p. C3.

194

28. Quoted in William F. Powers, "Virtual Politics: Campaigning in Cyberspace," *Washington Post*, November 8, 1994, p. E1.

29. Wayne Rash, Jr., *Politics on the Nets* (New York: Freeman, 1997), 81.

30. For a matrix of communication techniques, see Goldenberg and Traugott, *Campaigning for Congress*, 113–14.

31. Peter C. Clemente, *State of the Net: The New Frontier* (New York: McGraw-Hill, 1998), 53.

32. Find/SVP at http://wtrg.finsvp.com/index.html; "Internet Market Share Size and Demographics: A Survey by Wirthlin Worldwide and WSI," September 1996, and "One-in-Ten Voters Online for Campaign '96," Pew

Research Center for the People and the Press, at http://www.people-press.org/ tech96sum.htm.

33. Quoted in Barbara J. Saffir, "Weaving Their Web: The Candidates Race to Cyberspace," *Washington Post*, July 23, 1995, p. C3.

34. For a discussion of the creation of a White House Web site, see Gary Chapman, "Sending a Message to the White House," *Technology Review*, July 1993, p. 16; and Lorien Golaski, "Taking the Cyber Plunge: White House Sets Good Example," *Business Marketing*, April 1995, p. T-2.

35. Edmund L. Andrews, "The '96 Race on the Internet: Surfer Beware," *New York Times*, October 23, 1995, p. A1.

36. Telephone interview with Gary Torello, president of QGM and Web-master for the campaign site of Ed Munster, who ran in the 2d Congressional District in Connecticut, November 20, 1996.

37. Mark Hall, "One-to-One Politics in Cyberspace," *Media Studies Journal* 11 (Winter 1997): 97–103.

38. Personal interview with Lynn Reed, president of NetPoliticsGroup.com and former campaign staff member for Clinton/Gore in 1996 and Bill Bradley for President, November 17, 2000.

39. For a discussion of this coverage by online media Web sites, see Hall, "One-to-One Politics"; and Jane Singer, "A New Front Line in the Battle for Readers? Online Coverage of the 1996 Election by Denver's Competing Newspapers," *Electronic Journal of Communication* 7 (1997), at http://www.cios.org/www/ejcmain.htm.

40. See the July 1996 issue in particular.

41. Douglas Muzzio and David Birdsell, "The 1996 Net Voter," *Public Perspective*, December–January 1997, pp. 42–43.

42. Dave D'Alessio, "Use of the World Wide Web in the 1996 U.S. Election," *Electoral Studies* 16 (1997): 489–500.

43. Elaine Ciulla Kamarck, "Campaigning on the Internet in the Elections of 1998," in *Democracy.com? Governance in a Networked World*, ed. Elaine Ciulla Kamarck and Joseph S. Nye, Jr. (Hollis, N.H.: Hollis Publishing, 1999), 99–123.

44. Jeffrey D. Sadow and Karen James, "Virtual Billboards? Candidate Web Sites and Campaigning in 1998," paper delivered at the annual meeting of the American Political Science Association, Atlanta, Georgia, September 2–5, 1999.

45. Kamarck, "Campaigning on the Internet."

46. David A. Dulio, Donald L. Goff, and James A. Thurber, "Untangled Web: Internet Use during the 1998 Election," *PS: Political Science & Politics* 32 (March 1999): 53–59.

47. For a discussion of Jesse Ventura's campaign's use of the Internet and e-mail in the 1998 Minnesota gubernatorial race, see Jennifer Stromer-Galley, "On-line Interaction and Why Candidates Avoid It," *Journal of Communica-*

tion 50 (Autumn 2000): 111–32; and Phil Madsen, "Notes Regarding Jesse Ventura's Internet Use in His 1998 Campaign for Minnesota Governor," at http://www.jesseventura.org/internet/netnotes.htm.

48. Robert V. Friedenberg, *Communication Consultants in Political Campaigns: Ballot Box Warriors* (Westport, Conn.: Praeger, 1997), 205.

49. Corrado and Firestone, *Elections in Cyberspace*, 12.

50. Kamarck, "Campaigning on the Internet."

51. Ron Faucheux, "How Campaigns Are Using the Internet: An Exclusive Nationwide Survey," *Campaigns & Elections*, September 1998, pp. 22–25.

52. Ibid.

53. Ibid.

54. Quoted in Kamarck, "Campaigning on the Internet," 107–8.

55. Ibid., 108–11.

56. Ibid., 112–14.

57. Dulio, Goff, and Thurber, "Untangled Web: Internet Use during the 1998 Election," 54–55.

58. Kamarck, "Campaigning on the Internet," 114–16.

59. Faucheux, "How Campaigns Are Using the Internet," 22.

60. See Stromer-Galley, "On-line Interaction and Why Candidates Avoid It"; and Madsen, "Notes regarding Jesse Ventura's Internet Use in His 1998 Campaign for Minnesota Governor."

61. Dulio, Goff, and Thurber, "Untangled Web," 54–55.

62. Ibid., 54.

63. An ABC News/*Washington Post* poll, July 25, 2000, showed Bush leading Gore 51 percent to 45 percent among likely voters. A postconvention poll reported August 7, 2000, by CNN/*USA Today*/*Time* showed Bush at 54 percent to Gore's 37 percent among likely voters.

64. A CNN/*USA Today*/*Time* poll on August 20 showed Gore at 47 percent and Bush at 46 percent; a *New York Times*/CBS poll on September 12 showed Gore leading Bush 46 percent to 43 percent among likely voters, with 9 percent undecided; an ABC News/*Washington Post* poll on October 16 put Bush at 48 percent and Gore at 44 percent, and on November 6, they were at 48 percent and 45 percent, respectively.

65. Gallup Organization, "Presidential Poll, Oct. 31–Nov. 2, 2000," at http://www.gallup.com/poll/releases/pr001103.asp.

66. *USA Today*, at http://www.usatoday.com/news/e98/e3152.htm.

67. Darrell West, *Air Wars: Television Advertising in Election Campaigns, 1952–2000*, 3d ed. (Washington, D.C.: CQ Press, 2001).

68. Ibid.

69. Gerald Pomper et al., *The Election of 2000* (New York: Chatham House, 2001); James W. Ceaser and Andrew E. Busch, *The Perfect Tie: The True Story of the 2000 Presidential Election* (New York: Rowman & Littlefield, 2001).

70. Pomper et al., *The Election of 2000*.

71. West, *Air Wars.*

72. West shows that the comparative emphases on personalities and issues have varied across elections. The elections of 1960, 1976, and 1980 represent high marks in the advertising of personal characteristics by candidates. See West, *Air Wars.*

73. Jo Mannies, "Carnahan Campaign's Last 3 Weeks Were History in the Making: Manager Says Election Boiled Down to Values," *St. Louis Post-Dispatch*, November 9, 2000, p. A1.

74. Terry Ganey and Jon Sawyer, "Behind-the-Scenes Players Saw Only One Option for Senate: Jean Carnahan," *St. Louis Post-Dispatch*, December 31, 2000, p. A1.

75. Jo Mannies, "With 6 Months to Go, Talent Is Running Ads in Campaign for Governor: Contest Hasn't Generated Interest, at Least in Missouri," *St. Louis Post-Dispatch*, April 27, 2000, p. A1.

76. Virginia Young, "Candidates for Governor Aren't Going Down the Low Road: Despite Being Little-Known, Democrat Holden, GOP Rival Talent Avoid Attacks," *St. Louis Post-Dispatch*, September 25, 2000, p. A1.

77. Kit Wagar, "Holden Is Close to Win in Tight Race for Governor," *Kansas City Star*, November 8, 2000, p. A1.

78. Eric Stern, "Post-Dispatch Ad Check: Steve Gaw," *St. Louis Post-Dispatch*, October 31, 2000, p. B4.

79. Dulio, Goff, and Thurber, "Untangled Web," 58.

80. Quoted in Pete Engardio, "Activists without Borders: The Net Is Changing the Rules of Power Politics," *Business Week*, October 4, 1999, p. 148.

81. David C. King, "Catching Voters in the Web," in Kamarck and Nye, *Democracy.com?* 126.

82. "One-in-Ten Voters," at http://www.people-press.org/tech96sum.htm.

83. "The Tough Job of Communicating with Voters," Pew Research Center for the People and the Press, February 5, 2000, at http://www.people-press .org/jan00rpt2.htm.

84. Richard L. Berke, "Forbes Declares Candidacy on Internet and the Stump," *New York Times*, March 17, 1999, p. A19.

85. Amy Borrus, "On the Stump, Online," *Business Week*, April 12, 1999, p. 123; and Engardio, "Activists without Borders," p. 148.

86. Rebecca Fairley Raney, "FEC Allows Matching Funds for Online Donations," *New York Times*, June 10, 1999, at http://www.politicsonline.com/ coverage/nytimes4/index.html.

87. Engardio, "Activists without Borders," p. 148; and "Online Fundraising," *USA Today*, October 12, 1999, p. 1A.

88. Michael Isikoff, "How He's Catching a Cash Wave," *Newsweek*, February 14, 2000, p. 35.

89. Anthony Corrado, "Financing the 2000 Elections," in Pomper et al., *The Election of 2000*, 102.

90. Don Lewicki and Tim Ziaukas, "The Digital Tea Leaves of Election 2000: The Internet and the Future of Presidential Politics," *First Monday* 5 (December 2000), at http://firstmonday.org/issues/issue5_12/lewicki/index. html.

91. Personal interview with Ben Green, Webmaster for the Gore/Lieberman campaign, March 1, 2001; and "Bush Funds Top $80 Million," *New York Times*, April 15, 2000, p. A10.

92. Anthony DePalma, "Meet, Greet and Collect Online," *New York Times*, April 2, 2000, sec. 3, p. 2.

93. Engardio, "Activists without Borders," p. 148.

94. Personal interview with Lynn Reed, president of NetPoliticsGroup.com and former campaign staff member for Clinton/Gore in 1996 and Bill Bradley for President, November 17, 2000.

95. Ibid.

96. Ibid., and telephone interview with Cliff Angelo, Webmaster for the George W. Bush for President Campaign, December 22, 2000.

97. Leslie Wayne, "E-Mail Part of the Effort to Turn Out the Voters," *New York Times*, November 6, 2000, p. C6.

98. Reed interview.

99. See Robert Cwiklik, "Web Soapboxes Run into Rules for Old Media," *Wall Street Journal*, November 11, 1999, p. B1; and Patti Harrigan, "Web-site Parody Gets Bush Reaction," *Boston Globe*, June 18, 1999, p. D4.

100. Quoted in Borrus, "On the Stump, Online," p. 123.

Chapter 3

1. For a discussion of candidate electoral strategies, see Paul S. Herrnson, ed., *Playing Hardball: Campaigning for the U.S. Congress* (Upper Saddle River, N.J.: Prentice Hall, 2001); Michael Bailey et al., eds., *Campaigns & Elections: Contemporary Case Studies* (Washington, D.C.: CQ Press, 2000); James A. Thurber and Candice J. Nelson, eds., *Campaigns & Elections American Style* (Boulder, Colo.: Westview, 1995); and Barbara G. Salmore and Stephen A. Salmore, *Candidates, Parties, and Campaigns: Electoral Politics in America*, 2d ed. (Washington, D.C.: CQ Press, 1989).

2. Figures from Kathleen Jamieson, *Packaging the Presidency*, 2d ed. (New York: Oxford University Press, 1992), cited in Darrell West, *Air Wars: Television Advertising in Election Campaigns, 1952–2000* (Washington, D.C.: CQ Press, 2001).

3. Salmore and Salmore, *Candidates, Parties, and Campaigns*, 11.

4. Ibid., and Herrnson, *Playing Hardball*, 6–7.

5. For a discussion of vice-presidential liabilities in running a presidential campaign, see Nelson W. Polsby and Aaron Wildavsky, *Presidential Elections: Strategies and Structures of American Politics*, 10th ed. (New York: Chatham, 2000), 87–93.

6. For an example of how this phenomenon occurred in the 2000 presidential election, see Marjorie Randon Hershey, "The Campaign and the Media," in Pomper et al., *Election of 2000*, 46–72; and Erika Falk and Sean Aday, "Are Voluntary Standards Working? Candidate Discourse on Network Evening News Programs," Annenberg Public Policy Center report, December 20, 2000, at http://www.appcpenn.org/Candidate_Discourse/2000-general-report-final.htm.

7. James A. Thurber, "The Transformation of American Campaigns," in Thurber and Nelson, *Campaigns & Elections American Style*, 4.

8. Cass Sunstein, *Republic.com* (Princeton, N.J.: Princeton University Press, 2001), 80–84.

9. Telephone interview with Cliff Angelo, Webmaster for the George W. Bush for President Campaign, December 22, 2000.

10. Ibid.

11. Personal interview with Senator John McCain, December 9, 2000.

12. Angelo interview.

13. Personal interview with Ben Green, Webmaster for the Gore/Lieberman campaign, March 1, 2001.

14. Ibid.

15. Angelo interview.

16. Green interview.

17. Personal interview with Sarah Howard of the Carnahan for Senate Campaign, October 7, 2000.

18. Green interview.

19. Ibid.

20. Ibid.

21. Personal interview with Katie Maccracken, press secretary, Holden for (Missouri) Governor Campaign, November 14, 2000.

22. Howard interview.

23. Personal interview with Tim Haley, campaign manager for Buchanan/Foster 2000, November 20, 2000.

24. Don Lewicki and Tim Ziaukas, "The Digital Tea Leaves of Election 2000: The Internet and the Future of Presidential Politics," *First Monday* 5 (December 2000), at http://firstmonday.org/issues/issue5_12/lewicki/index.html.

25. Personal interview with Jonah Baker, Webmaster for Ralph Nader for President, November 17, 2000.

26. Curtis J. Sitomer, "Jesse Unruh: A Devotee of Politics and Power," *Christian Science Monitor*, August 13, 1987, p. 17.

27. Rajiv Chandrasekaran, "Politics Finding a Home on the Net," *Washington Post*, November 22, 1996, p. A4.

28. Martin Kettle, "Bradley Uses Web to Snare Votes," *Guardian*, January 18, 2000, p. 13.

29. Personal interview with Jason Braswell, Webmaster for Buchanan/Foster 2000, November 20, 2000.

30. Baker interview.

31. Green interview.

32. Telephone interview with Brett Thompson, Webmaster for the Talent for Governor Campaign, October 11, 2000.

33. Ibid.

34. Andrew Miga, "Campaign 2000: Bush Camp Launches Grassroots Media Blitz," *Boston Herald*, October 31, 2000, p. 5.

35. James Dao, "The 2000 Campaign: The Voters; Ringing Phones, Chiming Doorbells, Stuffed E-Mailboxes: The Great Voter Roundup," *New York Times*, November 7, 2000, p. A22.

36. Angelo interview.

37. Dao, "The 2000 Campaign."

38. Quoted in Leslie Wayne, "E-Mail Part of the Effort to Turn Out the Voters," *New York Times*, November 6, 2000, p. C6.

39. See, for example, Charles Bowen, "Campaign 2000: The Internet's Political Impact," *Editor & Publisher*, October 2, 1999, p. 29.

40. See Timothy Crouse, *The Boys on the Bus* (New York: Random House, 1973).

41. Wayne Rash, Jr., *Politics on the Nets* (New York: Freeman, 1997), 118.

42. Baker interview.

43. Howard interview.

44. Green interview.

45. Ibid.

46. Quoted in Lewicki and Ziaukas, "Digital Tea Leaves of Election 2000."

47. Erving Goffman, *The Presentation of Self in Everyday Life* (New York: Doubleday, 1959), 4.

48. For some discussion of the concept of self-presentation, see ibid. and Mark R. Leary, *Self-Presentation: Impression Management and Interpersonal Behavior* (Madison, Wis.: Brown & Benchmark, 1995).

49. Leary, *Self-Presentation*, 5.

50. Ibid., 80–85.

51. For a discussion of candidates' presentation of self in the congressional context, see Richard Fenno, *Homestyle: House Members in Their Districts* (Boston: Little, Brown, 1978), 54–135.

52. For a discussion of political communication during this period, see Culver Smith, *The Press, Politics, and Patronage* (Athens: University of Georgia Press, 1977); and Frank Luther Mott, *Jefferson and the Press* (Baton Rouge: Louisiana State University Press, 1943).

53. See Edward W. Chester, *Radio, Television, and American Politics* (New York: Sheed and Ward, 1969); Thomas E. Patterson, *The Mass Media Election* (New York: Praeger, 1980); Thomas E. Patterson, *Out of Order* (New York:

Knopf, 1993); Paula Tait, "Eight Myths of Video Cassette Campaigning," *Campaigns & Elections*, December 1993–January 1994; and Richard Davis and Diana Owen, *New Media and American Politics* (New York: Oxford University Press, 1998), chap. 9.

54. Salmore and Salmore, *Candidates, Parties, and Campaigns*, 111–37.

55. Green interview.

56. See David W. Moore, "In Presidential Race, Leadership Appears to Be Key," Gallup News Service, January 21, 2000, at http://www.gallup.com/poll/releases/pr000121.asp; and "Gore Issue Edge Less Potent," Pew Research Center for the People and the Press, November 1, 2000, at http://www.people-press.org/loct00rpt.htm.

57. Richard Davis, *The Web of Politics: The Internet's Impact on the American Political System* (New York: Oxford University Press, 1999), 111.

58. Quoted in Carolyn Said, "Politically Connected: Bush, Campaigns Plug into Net to Reach Voters, Organize Volunteers," *San Francisco Chronicle*, October 9, 2000, p. D1.

59. Elaine Ciulla Kamarck, "Campaigning on the Internet in the Elections of 1998," in *Democracy.com? Governance in a Networked World*, ed. Elaine Ciulla Kamarck and Joseph S. Nye, Jr. (Hollis, N.H.: Hollis Publishing, 1999), 99–123.

60. Philip Howard and Lee Rainie, "The Revolution That Hasn't Yet Begun," *IMP: Information Impacts Magazine*, May 2000, at http://www.cisp.org/imp/may_2000/05_00rainie-insight.htm.

61. Elizabeth Weise, "Not Yet for the Net," *Media Studies Journal* 14 (Winter 2000): 36–41.

62. Don Van Natta, Jr., "Courting Web-Head Cash," *New York Times*, February 13, 2000, sec. 4, p. 4.

63. Rash, *Politics on the Nets*, 69.

64. Howard and Rainie, "The Revolution That Hasn't Yet Begun."

65. Thurber, "Transformation of American Campaigns," 3.

66. See, for example, Benjamin Page, *Choices and Echoes in Presidential Elections* (Chicago, Ill.: University of Chicago Press, 1978); Anthony Downs, *An Economic Theory of Democracy* (New York: Harper and Row, 1957); and Kenneth Shepsle, "The Strategy of Ambiguity: Uncertainty and Electoral Competition," *American Political Science Review* 66 (June 1972): 555–68.

67. Richard D. McKelvey and Peter C. Ordeshook, "Sequential Elections with Limited Information," *American Journal of Political Science* 29 (August 1985): 480–512; and Ronald B. Rapoport, Walter J. Stone, and Alan I. Abramowitz, "Do Endorsements Matter? Group Influence in the 1984 Democratic Caucuses," *American Political Science Review* 85 (March 1991): 193–203.

68. See Russell J. Dalton, Paul A. Beck, and Robert Huckfeldt, "Partisan Cues and the Media: Information Flows in the 1992 Presidential Election," *American Political Science Review* 92 (March 1998): 111–26; Lana Stein and

Arnold Fleischmann, "Newspaper and Business Endorsements in Municipal Elections: A Test of the Conventional Wisdom," *Journal of Urban Affairs* 9 (1987): 325–36; Steven Coombs, "Editorial Endorsements and Electoral Outcomes," in *More Than News: Media Power in Public Affairs*, ed. Michael Bruce MacKuen and Steven Lane Coombs (Beverly Hills, Calif.: Sage, 1981), 147–226; and Robert Erikson, "The Influence of Newspaper Endorsements in Presidential Elections," *American Journal of Political Science* 20 (May 1976): 207–34.

69. Thompson interview.

70. See Robert Klotz, "Virtual Criticism: Negative Advertising on the Internet in the 1996 Senate Races," *Political Communication* 15 (July 1998): 347–65; and Davis, *Web of Politics*, 102–4.

71. Kamarck, "Campaigning on the Internet"; and Davis, *Web of Politics*, 102–5.

72. West, *Air Wars*, 57–61.

Chapter 4

1. See the American National Election Studies, 2000, for figures on newspaper audiences.

2. See Bruce Bimber, "Measuring the Gender Gap on the Internet," *Social Science Quarterly* 81 (2000): 865–75; and Bruce Bimber, "The Internet and Citizen Communication with Government: Does the Medium Matter?" *Political Communication* 16 (1999): 409–28.

3. See National Telecommunications and Information Administration and Economics and Statistics Administration, U.S. Department of Commerce, "A Nation Online: How Americans Are Expanding Their Use of the Internet," 2002, at http://www.ntia.doc.gov/ntiahome/dn/html/Chapter3.htm; and "The Internet News Audience Goes Ordinary," Pew Research Center for the People and the Press, January 14, 1999, at http://people-press.org/reports.

4. 0.01 level.

5. U.S. Bureau of the Census, 1999.

6. In addition to our analysis of presidential and state-level Web audiences, we also included a limited analysis of three nonpartisan voter information sites: Freedom Channel, Project Vote Smart, and DemocracyNet. The purpose of that analysis was to make comparisons among audiences. We do not discuss the nonpartisan sites at any length in this book, because for the most part the basic data do not add much to the picture derived from looking at the candidate sites. Where a few interesting differences exist, we discuss these in notes to the main text. For example, people visiting the nonpartisan sites were younger by an average of three years than people visiting presidential Web sites; they were twice as likely to be a racial or ethnic minority; and they were more likely to be independents. In general, this finding is consistent with one of the stated missions of nonpartisan civic information providers,

such as Project Vote Smart, which is to provide information geared to younger voters. However, we note that the median age of 35 (versus 38 for the candidates' sites) hardly indicates a substantial youth appeal. The fact that nonpartisan sites were more likely to attract independents than the candidates' own sites is consistent with our theoretical expectations, which predicted that partisans tend to seek partisan information, particularly for reinforcement. Conversely, nonpartisans are more likely to seek nonpartisan information through the Internet.

7. Significant at the 0.05 level.

8. This difference represents about half of a standard deviation and is significant at the 0.01 level.

9. When we compared people who saw a presidential Web site with those who saw a nonpartisan site, we found the nonpartisan audience to be slightly less knowledgeable, by an average of a half point.

10. Significant at the 0.01 level.

11. Diana C. Mutz and Paul S. Martin, "Facilitating Communication across Lines of Political Difference: The Role of Mass Media," *American Political Science Review* 95, no.1 (2001): 97–114.

Chapter 5

1. Our approach to measuring the effects of Web sites on their audiences reflected the fact that assessing how any one factor or phenomenon affects human thinking or behavior is a challenge. It is one thing to use surveys to obtain descriptive evidence about who the members of an audience are and quite another to make inferences about how that audience was affected by a Web site. In general, two approaches to this problem are available: asking people to explain how they were affected and directly observing how people's behavior changes. In both cases, one of the main challenges is isolating the effects of the one factor of interest from all of the other influences on people's lives and actions. In our surveys, we asked people to tell us whether they had gone back to a candidate Web site a second time or more and also whether they felt they were influenced by the Web site or sites that they had seen. We also compared what people who had seen a site told us about themselves politically with what we were told by those who had not. We were able to draw some inferences from what people told us, but we also relied upon our laboratory experiment to help us overcome the problems of recall and self-perception that occur in surveys. In our experiment, we were able to survey people, let them visit a Web site under controlled conditions, and then survey them again immediately. Where we found a change in knowledge or a change in feelings about candidates, we were generally able to ascribe that change to something that happened in the experiment.

2. Within each site's audience, we found some interesting variations on the basic themes of education and strength of partisanship as influences on

return visits. Al Gore's site had a gender effect that we found at none of the other sites. Men were less likely to recall a return to Gore's site than women and were also less likely to remember than men visiting the other sites in our survey. About 45 percent of men who visited at least once returned to the Gore site, compared with 55 percent of women and 57 percent of men at Bush's site, a difference that is statistically significant at the 0.05 level. Gore's site also produced an age effect that we found at none of the other sites. Returning visitors were on average four years older (41) than one-time visitors, also significant at the 0.05 level.

3. This difference is statistically significant at the 0.01 level.

4. Statistically significant at the 0.01 level. The standard deviation among the Web audience is 1.65, so return visitors scored about one-third of a standard deviation better than one-time visitors.

5. Our measure of knowledge for this question was a brief objective test administered before the subjects visited the Web sites and again after. On this test, we did not try to assess subjects' factual knowledge about specific issues or about candidates' positions. Instead, we inquired about a few basic aspects of the electoral process and about the presidential candidates, including questions about how far away the election was in weeks, whether there was a Senate election in their state and whether the subject could name the candidates, whether there was an election for governor, how many years Al Gore had been vice president, and what job George Bush held while running. The purpose was to see whether these generic forms of campaign-related knowledge would be affected by the experience of viewing Web sites under laboratory conditions. This knowledge test therefore differed from the even more generic knowledge test we used in our surveys.

6. We defined "doing better" as improving one's score by one correct question or more. Our research design did not include control subjects who did not view any Web site and only took the knowledge tests.

7. Statistically significant at the 0.05 level. This is especially important substantively, since our subjective knowledge test contained several items oriented toward the presidential election.

8. John Zaller, *The Nature and Origins of Mass Opinion* (Cambridge: Cambridge University Press, 1992). Also see W. Russell Neuman, *The Paradox of Mass Politics: Knowledge and Opinion in the American Electorate* (Cambridge, Mass.: Harvard University Press, 1986).

9. Measuring changes in feeling is especially difficult, since it involves assessing a very subjective characteristic. Again, we combined survey research and our laboratory experiment to look at feelings in two main ways: simply as support or opposition to a candidate and as a measure of the strength of support or opposition. In our surveys, we asked people to recall their feelings about each candidate whose site they visited before that first visit, and then again after.

10. Chi Sq.=7.8, p=0.02.

11. Chi Sq.=14.1, p<.01.

12. Chi Sq.=11.4, p<.01.

13. Establishing with certainty whether the Web experience affected voting is even more difficult than assessing feeling effects. Laboratory experiments are not up to the task, since it is not possible to present people an actual opportunity to vote as part of the experiment, except in a purely hypothetical way. Asking people in an experiment about their feelings must be done carefully, but there is simply no reliable way to ask people to extrapolate to voting day and report in any meaningful way whether looking at the Web site in the experiment will affect their later propensity to vote; whatever answers people gave would be highly unreliable. Making informed inferences about the effects of Web sites on voting requires what is called a panel survey, where voters are questioned about their experiences at some point prior to election day and then the same group of voters is then resurveyed after election day. The first wave provides an assessment of Web experiences and general inclination to vote, and the second wave provides an indicator of whether people actually did vote. By comparing answers for the same individual people, it is possible to draw some strongly suggestive conclusions. This was our approach.

14. The figure of 84 percent undoubtedly reflects both a higher turnout rate and the well-known propensity of people taking surveys to overreport voting.

15. Chi Sq.=0.56, p=0.78.

16. Logistic regression model available upon request. Model Chi Sq.=32, p=0.004; Nagelkerke R^2=0.39.

Chapter 6

1. For a discussion, see Maxwell E. McCombs and Donald L. Shaw, "The Agenda-Setting Function of the Mass Media," *Public Opinion Quarterly* 36 (1972): 176–87; Donald L. Shaw and Maxwell McCombs, *Emergence of American Political Issues* (St. Paul, Minn.: West, 1977); George R. Funkhouser, "The Issues of the Sixties: An Exploratory Study in the Dynamics of Public Opinion," *Public Opinion Quarterly* 37 (1973): 62–75; Shanto Iyengar and Donald R. Kinder, *News That Matters* (Chicago, Ill.: University of Chicago Press, 1987); Shanto Iyengar et al., "Experimental Demonstrations of the 'Not So Minimal' Consequences of Television News Programs," *American Political Science Review* 81 (1982): 848–58; and David L. Protess and Maxwell McCombs, *Agenda Setting: Readings on Media, Public Opinion, and Policymaking* (Hillsdale, N.J.: Erlbaum, 1991).

2. For discussions of these effects, see, for example, Iyengar and Kinder, *News That Matters*; and Thomas E. Patterson, *Out of Order* (New York: Knopf, 1993).

3. Nicholas A. Valentino, Vincent L. Hutchings, and Ismail K. White, "Cues That Matter: How Political Ads Prime Racial Attitudes," *American Political Science Review* 96, no. 1 (2002): 75–90.

4. Walter Lippmann. *Drift and Mastery* (New York: Mitchell Mennerly, 1914).

5. For a discussion of selectivity, see David Sears and Jonathan Freedman, "Selective Exposure to Information: A Critical Review," *Public Opinion Quarterly* 31 (Summer 1967): 194–213. For samples of research suggesting selective exposure and selective attention, see Jay G. Blumler and Denis G. McQuail, *Television in Politics* (Chicago, Ill.: University of Chicago Press, 1969); Thomas E. Patterson and Robert D. McClure, *The Unseeing Eye: The Myth of Television Power in National Elections* (New York: Putnam, 1976); Thomas E. Patterson, *The Mass Media Election* (New York: Praeger, 1980); and Diana Owen, *Media Messages in American Presidential Elections* (Westport, Conn.: Greenwood, 1991).

6. Charles Tabor and Milton Lodge, "Motivated Skepticism in the Evaluation of Political Beliefs," paper prepared for presentation at the annual meeting of the American Political Science Association, Atlanta, Ga., Sept. 2–5, 1999; Diana C. Mutz and Paul S. Martin, "Facilitating Communication across Lines of Political Difference: The Role of Mass Media," *American Political Science Review* 95, no. 1 (2001): 97–114; and Charles Lord, M. Ross, and Mark Lepper, "Biased Assimilation and Attitude Polarization: The Effects of Prior Theories on Subsequently Considered Evidence," *Journal of Personality and Social Psychology* 27 (1979): 2098–109.

7. Shanto Iyengar, Kyu Hahn, and Markus Prior, "Has Technology Made Attention to Political Campaigns More Selective? An Experimental Study of the 2000 Campaign," paper prepared for presentation at the annual meeting of the American Political Science Association, San Francisco, September 2, 2001.

8. Tabor and Lodge, "Motivated Skepticism in the Evaluation of Political Beliefs."

9. Paul Allen Beck et al., "The Social Calculus of Voting: Interpersonal, Media, and Organizational Influences on Presidential Choices," *American Political Science Review* 96, no. 1 (2002): 57–73; and Robert P. Vallone, Lee Ross, and Mark R. Lepper, "The Hostile Media Phenomenon: Biased Perceptions and Perceptions of Media Bias in Coverage of the Beirut Massacre," *Journal of Personality and Social Psychology* 49, no. 3 (1985): 577–85.

10. Mutz and Martin, "Facilitating Communication across Lines of Political Difference."

11. Stephen Ansolabehere and Shanto Iyengar, *Going Negative: How Political Advertisements Shrink and Polarize the Electorate* (New York: Free Press, 1995).

12. Tabor and Lodge, "Motivated Skepticism in the Evaluation of Political Beliefs."

13. Michael MacKuen, W. Russell Neuman, and George E. Marcus, "Affective Intelligence, Voting, and Matters of Public Policy," paper prepared for presentation at the annual meeting of the American Political Science Association, Washington, D.C., Aug. 31–Sept. 3, 2000.

14. Mutz and Martin, "Facilitating Communication across Lines of Political Difference."

15. Ibid.

16. W. Russell Neuman, *The Future of the Mass Audience* (Cambridge: Cambridge University Press, 1990); Mutz and Martin, "Facilitating Communication across Lines of Political Difference"; Iyengar, Hahn, and Prior, "Has Technology Made Attention to Political Campaigns More Selective?" and Cass Sunstein, *Republic.com* (Princeton, N.J.: Princeton University Press, 2001).

17. For an explicit comparison of selectivity between computer-based media and other types, see Iyengar, Hahn, and Prior, "Has Technology Made Attention to Political Campaigns More Selective?" Using a quasi-experimental approach, they found that citizens explored computer-based campaign materials in ways generally consistent with the theory of selectivity. In their study, selectivity on the basis of partisanship was quite low, though higher among Republicans and conservatives than among Democrats and liberals. Issue selectivity was much stronger, as citizens tended to pay most attention to issues relevant to their own concerns.

18. Iyengar, Hahn, and Prior, "Has Technology Made Attention to Political Campaigns More Selective?" and Mutz and Martin, "Facilitating Communication across Lines of Political Difference."

19. Curtis Gans, "The Internet Will Offer New Ways to Avoid Public Affairs," *Political Standard*, May–June 1999, at http://www.bettercampaigns.org/STANDARD/junectrpt.HTM.

20. These figures come from a variety of surveys conducted by several organizations. They are discussed in Michael Delli Carpini and Scott Keeter, *What Americans Know about Politics and Why It Matters* (New Haven, Conn.: Yale University Press, 1996).

21. For an excellent discussion of the strategic dynamics of political knowledge and attentiveness, see R. Douglas Arnold, *The Logic of Congressional Action* (New Haven, Conn.: Yale University Press, 1991).

22. Michael Cornfield, "A User's Guide to the 'Digital Divide,'" *Campaigns & Elections*, April 2000, p. 47.

23. Quoted in Martin Kettle, "Bradley Uses Web to Snare Votes," *Guardian*, January 18, 2000, p. 13.

24. Michael Cornfield, "Philadelphia: The Political Convention Rewired,"

Vanishing Voter Project, at http://www.vanishingvoter.org/releases/08–13–0 internet-2.shtml; and Thomas E. Patterson, "A Tale of the Missing Audience," Vanishing Voter Project, at http://www.vanishingvoter.org/releases/08-13 -00conv-3.shtml.

25. Ansolabehere and Iyengar, *Going Negative*.

26. For historical narratives of the role of the penny press, see Michael Schudson, *Discovering the News* (New York: Basic, 1978); Frank Luther Mott, *American Journalism: A History, 1690–1960* (New York: Macmillan, 1962); and Alfred McClung Lee, *The Daily Newspaper in America* (New York: Macmillan, 1937).

27. See Richard Hofstadter, *The Age of Reform* (New York: Vintage, 1955).

28. Michael Schudson, *The Good Citizen* (Cambridge, Mass.: Harvard University Press, 1998).

29. C. Atkin et al., "Quality v. Quantity in Televised Political Advertisements," *Public Opinion Quarterly* 37 (1973): 209–24; Craig L. Brians and Martin P. Wattenberg, "Campaign Issue Knowledge and Salience: Comparing Reception from TV Commercials, TV News and Newspapers," *American Journal of Political Science* 40, no. 1 (1996): 172–93; Patterson and McClure, *The Unseeing Eye*; Michael Pfau et al., "Influence of Communication Modalities on Voters' Perceptions of Candidates during Presidential Primary Campaigns," *Journal of Communication* 45, no. 1 (1995): 122–33; and Darrell M. West, "Television Advertising in Election Campaigns," *Political Science Quarterly* 109, no. 5 (1995): 789–809. An important exception is X. Zhao and Steven Chaffee, "Campaign Advertisements versus Television News as Sources of Political Issue Information," *Public Opinion Quarterly* 59 (1995): 41–65.

30. C. Atkin and G. Heald, "Effects of Political Advertising," *Public Opinion Quarterly* 40 (1976): 212–28; C. Atkin et al., "Quality v. Quantity," 209–24; L. Bowen, "Time of Voting Decision and Use of Political Advertising: The Gorton, Slade Adams, Brock Senatorial Campaign," *Journalism Quarterly* 71, no. 3 (1994): 665–75.

31. Kim Friedkin Kahn and John Geer, "Creating Impressions: An Experimental Investigation of Political Advertising on Television," *Political Behavior* 16, no. 1 (1994): 93–116.

32. Ansolabehere and Iyengar, *Going Negative*.

33. On this topic, see Bimber, *Information and American Democracy: Technology in the Evolution of Political Power* (Cambridge: Cambridge University Press, 2002).

34. Personal interview with Caleb Weaver, deputy director of policy, Holden for (Missouri) Governor Campaign, November 14, 2000.

35. Patterson, *Out of Order*.

36. For a criticism of this approach by news media, see Thomas E. Patterson, "Doing Well and Doing Good: How Soft News and Critical Journalism Are Shrinking the News Audience and Weakening Democracy and What News

Outlets Can Do about It," Joan Shorenstein Center on the Press, Politics and Public Policy report, January 2001.

37. David Weinberger, *Small Pieces Loosely Joined: A Unified Theory of the Web* (Cambridge, Mass.: Perseus Books, 2002).

38. Sunstein, *Republic.com*, 26.

Appendix

1. For a discussion of the content analysis method as a social science research tool, see Ole R. Holsti, *Content Analysis for the Social Sciences and Humanities* (Reading, Mass.: Addison-Wesley, 1969); Thomas F. Carney, *Content Analysis: A Technique for Systematic Inference from Communications* (Winnipeg: University of Manitoba Press, 1972); Klaus Krippendorff, *Content Analysis: An Introduction to Its Methodology* (Beverly Hills, Calif.: Sage, 1980); and Arthur Asa Berger, *Media Research Techniques* (Newbury Park, Calif.: Sage, 1991).

2. Berger, *Media Research Techniques*, 28–29.

3. For a discussion of the computation of a composite reliability coefficient, see Holsti, *Content Analysis for the Social Sciences and Humanities*, 137–38.

4. Steve Jones, ed., *Doing Internet Research: Critical Issues and Methods for Examining the Net* (Thousand Oaks, Calif.: Sage, 1999), xii.

5. Stephen Ansolabehere and Shanto Iyengar, *Going Negative: How Political Advertisements Shrink and Polarize the Electorate* (New York: Free Press, 1995).

Acknowledgments

Conducting a research project of this size requires the talents and best efforts of many people. Our names are on the cover of *Campaigning Online*, but we realize that this book would not be in print were it not for the able assistance of many others. We are grateful to all of them for their support. We acknowledge the participation of five groups in the production of this book: colleagues whose ideas and advice assisted us; students and staff who labored with us to conduct the research; our research subjects and participants, whose experiences in the world of technology and politics comprise the evidence for this book; the funding organizations that made the work possible; and the staff at Oxford University Press.

A number of colleagues shared their wisdom and ideas, especially W. Russell Neuman, Michael X. Delli Carpini, Diana Owen, and Scott Keeter. We are most grateful to them for their collegiality.

The project employed an unusually large number of student assistants and other staff at various points along the way. At Brigham Young University, we thank Rachel Kirkland, Audrey Williams, Michael Dorrough, Gretchen Carr, Diane Parker, Robert Williamson, and Steve Bitner. At the University of California, Santa Barbara, we thank

Rob Patton, Diane Johnson, Joe Gardner, Robert Hinckley, Eric Patterson, and Lia Roberts. We also thank the staff of Wirthlin Worldwide, Inc., especially Dee Alsop and Justin Calapp, who conducted the survey research and who managed the experiments in San Diego, St. Louis, Charlotte, and New York.

This project entailed survey interviews with 2,500 people around the country and laboratory experiments involving 210 citizens who visited research facilities and spent an hour or so with us. We are very grateful for this enormous aggregate expenditure of time on the part of citizens who are increasingly harried by telemarketers and others requesting attention. In addition, in 2000, we interviewed staff of the major presidential campaigns and Missouri statewide races, to whom we are especially grateful for sharing their time with us, typically on more than one occasion, and trusting us with their views about how democracy works in the United States. In particular, we thank Ben Green, Cliff Angelo, Jonah Baker, Sarah Howard, and Brett Thompson.

This work was generously funded by the Carnegie Corporation of New York and the Pew Charitable Trusts. We appreciate their sincere interest in the substance of the questions and in our findings as well as their financial support.

Finally, we are grateful to the team at Oxford for their continued interest in our work. We particularly thank our editor, Dedi Felman, for her unfailing support along the way.

Acknowledgments

Index